Salk, Lee

Your child's
first year

H334 11.95

DATE DUE

DR. LEE SALK
YOUR CHILD'S
FIRST YEAR

CORNERSTONE LIBRARY

Published by Simon & Schuster, Inc.   *New York*

Copyright © 1983 by Dr. Lee Salk
All rights reserved
including the right of reproduction
in whole or in part in any form
Published by Cornerstone Library,
A Division of Simon & Schuster, Inc.
Simon & Schuster Building
1230 Avenue of the Americas
New York, New York 10020

CORNERSTONE LIBRARY and colophon are trademarks of Simon & Schuster, Inc.,
registered in the U.S. Patent and Trademark Office.

10 9 8 7 6 5 4 3 2 1
Manufactured in the United States of America

Library of Congress Cataloging in Publication Data

Salk, Lee, date.
  Your child's first year.

  Includes index.
  1. Infants. 2. Parenting. 3. Parent and child.
4. Family. I. Title.
HQ774.S23 1983   649'.122   83-7322
ISBN 0-346-12581-2

My appreciation to Deborah Katsh
for her helpful assistance in editing this book.

I dedicate this book to Mrs. Ann Houseal—
who has given so much of her love to her two children
and now to her two wonderful grandchildren.

CONTENTS

INTRODUCTION

PARENTHOOD HAS ALWAYS BEEN a rewarding but very difficult commitment. In the past, people generally did not give too much thought to whether or not they wanted to become parents. Young men and women reached a certain age, married, and bore children. Many of them consciously wanted to have children and eagerly awaited their arrival. Others probably would have chosen to remain childless but had families because it was expected of them. Some hoped for sons to inherit their farms or businesses or to carry on their names. Whatever the reason, their success or failure was based on instinct, interest, and the knowledge they had absorbed by watching their own mothers and fathers. No matter what the social and economic conditions, in good times and bad times, couples chose to have children with the idealistic, often naive belief that they "knew what was best for their baby."

The truth of the matter was that all too often they did not know what was best. They discovered too late that they had raised a daughter or son whose capacity to enjoy life, relationships, and work was severely limited. Traditionally, the accepted explanation for what went wrong was that "the kid just didn't want to make anything of himself" or "she was born that way—rotten."

Today we have a better understanding of how and why human beings turn out the way they do. We know that parents have a great influence on how their children turn out, a far greater influence on their children than they were previously credited with.

I have written this book in order to help you provide the best possible conditions for raising emotionally and physically healthy children. In more than twenty-five years as a practicing pediatric psychologist, I have learned a tremendous amount about parental concerns and anxieties. I have followed the progress of countless children from their prenatal life into their adolescence. I believe that parents need as much information as possible of the sort I have included. This information was not available to most of our parents and grandparents, and has been gathered after years of observing and listening to children. I feel that you as parents naturally want to protect and love your children, and I highly respect your desire to do so. But I do not think children can be raised by instinct alone.

In my classes for parents-to-be and new parents at the New York Hospital–Cornell Medical Center where I am Professor of Pediatrics and Professor of Psychology in Psychiatry, my purpose is to make clear how very important parents are in the lives of their babies. My hope is that, after reading this book, you will realize even more that your love and constant care in every aspect of your child's upbringing is the key to successful parenting.

There is no such thing as the perfect parent, and there never will be. Furthermore, there is no way you can get from one day to the next without encountering some predicament. My intention is to help you handle those problems more effectively. By sharing my insights with you, I hope to give you the necessary background so that you can trust yourself enough to relax and enjoy your new role— that of being a responsive and gratifying parent.

From the moment your baby is born he or she will be highly sensitive to you, your attitudes, and your reactions. Your task is to use that awareness to teach him to trust you. Be responsive to his needs, *all* his needs, whether by picking him up when he cries or by cuddling and sharing your life with him. You are helping your baby grow toward independence. Give him love and attention, and he will be prepared to accept the rules, regulations, and discipline that will safeguard his future health and happiness. Understand his infant priorities and your own, and that will help you instill in him better feelings about himself and others.

Along with our greater understanding of child development, we have seen many changes in people's attitudes. Today more couples are deciding not to have children because they do not want the "inconvenience," and some people would

rather divorce when a marriage goes bad than stay together and try to make the best of a bad situation the way they once would have. Newspapers and magazines often run articles about women's liberation and the effects it has had on family life. Women who chose to train for difficult professions are now asking themselves whether to work or be mothers and wondering whether it is possible to do both such important and demanding functions. Men are beginning to see that being a father means caring for and loving children and not just doling out allowances and punishments. People raising children alone is becoming more and more common. Some start out wanting to be single parents, and others may end up that way due to divorce or death.

I am happy to see that people are changing their views on what being a parent means. It makes possible changes from the old traditions of the woman having child-raising responsibility alone and the man staying out of the picture. Believing as I do that parenthood is the toughest job in the world, I have the highest respect for you for having elected the commitment of raising children. I hope to persuade all men and women to share responsibilities in every aspect of their babies' lives. What you give your baby in terms of your time and energy during the first year of life will be the basis of what happens throughout the rest of his years. I urge you not to underestimate the power and responsibilities of being a parent.

YOUR CHILD'S FIRST YEAR

1

CHOOSING
TO BE A PARENT

I BELIEVE THAT BECOMING A PARENT is the most important role a human being can undertake. As a psychologist treating people with emotional disorders, I have found that how you conduct yourself in life is affected to a very great extent by your earliest experiences. Over and over again I have traced my patients' difficulties or inabilities to function back to unfulfilled infantile and childhood needs.

Parental responsibility includes the prevention of possible emotional problems, and most of the parents of these patients are well-meaning people. They simply did not know how to provide their children with the emotional stability to cope with the stresses of everyday life. Some of them had been misguided by professionals whose experience did not include day-to-day observation of children. Others had accepted without question the prejudices of their parents. My hope is that I will be able to help you establish your own positive approach to child rearing.

Parents have the capacity to turn their children into angry, bitter adults or to bring them up to be emotionally healthy, useful members of society. Unfortunately, too often people slip into the role of parent without giving consideration to what it involves. By the time they have a child, they recognize that they might

have been better off had they not undertaken parenthood in the first place. By then it's too late, and it is the children who suffer most. Because of this, I think people should be educated about what parenthood involves, both its positive and negative aspects.

In a sense, all living things want to reproduce themselves; for human beings parenthood is more of a choice among other choices. Now that you have chosen to become a parent, your next task is to prepare yourself for making intelligent, informed decisions about how to raise a happy, trusting child.

When I was in the first grade, my teacher defined the necessities of life as food, clothing, and shelter. Over the years I have added a fourth one, the care of the young. Perhaps schools should offer a course in human survival training that covers parenthood education as well as the other necessities of life. We could thereby provide young people with the information necessary to cope effectively with their future responsibilities. Such a program would prepare them for parenthood, its problems, and its pleasures.

I consider parenthood to be not just motherhood but fatherhood as well. I strongly believe that both young men and women should be educated to be parents. For hundreds of years men have been discouraged from taking an active role in child rearing. The traditional father takes care of the bills and fixes the broken windows. In effect, it's like saying he pays his wife to raise his children for him. This is an unhealthy attitude, both from the point of view of a child's development and of parental satisfaction. It deprives both father and child of that very special and rewarding relationship with each other.

I suggest that we eliminate the separation of certain roles associated with men from those associated with women. Women should be encouraged to plan their lives to include not just the possibility of parenthood, but also the independence they can achieve by preparing for a profession or vocation. This is particularly important in the event of divorce or if there is a need for a second income to meet household expenses.

There is nothing wrong with the traditional approach of the wife staying home to cook and clean the house while the husband goes off to work. But I certainly would like to see both parents capable of changing roles periodically to relieve each other. There is no reason why a father cannot get up in the middle of the night and help a crying baby fall back to sleep, to diaper and feed her and be there to minister to her needs. Being tender and loving is just as much a male as a female responsibility. Either parent should be able to bathe the baby, and for a man to feel that this is unmasculine means he is cheating himself of a wonderful,

natural way to forge the bond between him and his baby. Parenthood is such a marvelous privilege. Why not have mother and father sharing it equally? If one parent cannot provide proper care because of illness or for any other reason, the other should be prepared to take over effectively.

Not too long ago in one of my new parent classes, a young father explained that he had been a truck driver and he had hurt his back. He was no longer able to drive a truck and was receiving disability compensation for the injury. When he decided to stay home with his baby and become a househusband, do the cooking, and take care of the household chores, his wife was delighted to have the opportunity to go back to her job as a schoolteacher. The setup worked out extremely well. The father was very much enjoying meeting a new and different sort of challenge, and his pleasure in his child was evident from the way in which he took care of her. As this large, muscular man held his baby tenderly in one of his enormous hands, she was obviously thrilled and cooed while gazing happily at him. There was great love and affection that passed between them.

I am often asked whether this sort of role exchange does not cause confusion in children. I have never yet seen this to be the case. As long as children have their emotional needs met at all the stages of their development, there will be no problems.

Why shouldn't children, after all, have the opportunity for two people rather than one to be responsible for their lives? A child who spends all of his or her time with the mother is more inclined to adopt her attitudes, habits, and mannerisms rather than those of both parents. Many people will argue that fathers are important so that sons can learn to identify with a male figure. I think it is essential for fathers to be involved with daughters as well. There is nothing wrong with a girl having ideas or values like her father or for a boy having ideas and values like his mother. Too often fathers are there physically but not emotionally and do not participate in raising their children. Only by having both active fathers and mothers can we teach our children to share in raising their children and know what it's like to be mothers and fathers.

Parenthood is very time-consuming and carries with it many emotional and financial burdens. You will discover, if you don't already know, that babies are helpless and totally dependent upon you to gratify their needs. Gone are the days when you could simply pick up and go someplace without any sort of preparation. A two-hour visit with friends or a walk in the park requires that you take along a great deal of equipment. You may find you are too tired to do many of the things you used to enjoy. Your relationships with other people will probably undergo changes. If you are the first among your friends to become parents, you may be looked upon strangely and perhaps even be excluded by them.

Many people, because of their own interest in becoming parents, assume that the rest of the world eagerly awaits them and their children. Finding an apartment that will rent to parents with youngsters may suddenly begin to seem like an impossibility. Parents accompanied by children are often kept waiting at restaurants or seated at out-of-the-way tables. Becoming a parent, I hasten to emphasize, is not simply a matter of taking on new responsibilities or being faced with inconveniences. There is an enormous amount of pleasure and fulfillment that offsets the problems.

As you and your child become better acquainted over the years, the mutual love and satisfaction will continue to flower. In a sense your relationship with your baby begins the moment a woman discovers she is pregnant. This is certainly true of the mother who can actually feel the fetus moving about in her womb, kicking or hiccuping. But it is more than likely that both of you will fantasize about what your lives will be like after your baby is born.

You will probably experience many different emotions. At times you will be very excited about how wonderful life will be after the birth of your beautiful baby. You may also have moments of panic when you wonder how you ever got yourself into this situation and whether you are doing the right thing by having a baby at this point in your life.

I have seen countless different combinations of parental reactions before the birth of a child. Some fathers are exuberant about the prospect while the mothers seem rather indifferent for a while. The reverse also happens frequently—the mother shows great excitement and gets wrapped in preparations for the infant. The father doesn't seem to care very much. Treating the pregnancy as if it is a nuisance, he cannot understand why his wife is so concerned.

Differences in the feelings couples have about the pregnancy can sometimes cause conflict. Each person wants the other to feel exactly as he or she does. Eventually these feelings work themselves out. Just because one parent does not seem to be as excited as the other at the outset does not mean that he or she will not be as responsive to the baby later on.

Some of your concerns are due to the fact that you are now going to be a parent and will have new responsibilities. You will find yourself wondering: Will I be a good parent? Will my child love me? How will I communicate with my newborn baby? Will we have enough money to buy what he needs? What if my baby becomes sick? What if my baby dies? All these thoughts are perfectly normal. Many of them are based on reality and the understandable worry you have about taking on a tremendous obligation.

Remember, too, that the intense and varying emotions you experience during pregnancy are not all due to your psychological reactions but also the physical changes that are taking place in the mother's body because of the pregnancy. At times you may feel marvelous and full of energy. People may comment on the glow you have about you. At other times you will be nauseated and tired or feel clumsy and unattractive.

Toward the end of the pregnancy women sometimes develop a good deal of anxiety about the labor and delivery. Many of your nighttime dreams may reflect precisely that. Parents begin to wonder whether or not their baby will be normal or whether she will have some sort of defect. It is interesting that in many films that depict the birth of a baby we see the doctor turning to the mother immediately after delivery and telling her, "Your baby is fine."

"Is my baby all right?" is one of the first questions so many parents ask in the delivery room. Don't be embarrassed by your concern. It makes sense and doesn't imply that you are overly anxious or not capable of being a good parent. Unless you accept your negative feelings, you eventually may find that your anxiety has built up to the point that you are resenting your spouse and baby. If you have been able to talk openly about your mixed feelings, you will be able to come to terms with them.

When you announce to your friends and relatives that you are pregnant, you may suddenly begin to hear horror stories. It seems strange to find that your friends or close relatives may do this to you. They will share with you rather grotesque stories about a baby who recently was born with a deformity or about some other tragedy that took place. What is so surprising is that people will tell you such tales at a time when you are already pregnant and there is not much you can do but listen and wonder what their motives are. Perhaps they are envious; on the other hand, they may have some notion that they are helping you face all the possibilities that lie ahead. Short of being rude, you probably will find it difficult to prevent these supposedly well-meaning friends from preparing you for the worst. Remember—hearing about other people's misfortunes does not make them come true for you.

You will also become the subject of a great deal of advice. It is amazing how many people will share all sorts of ideas and anecdotes, most of which somehow seem to undermine your self-confidence rather than making you feel more optimistic about your abilities. You can be sure that most of the advice you get will be contrary to your natural instincts.

You may be told that you should not reach for things because stretching can cause you to miscarry or that you should rest a lot. Obviously you should not move pianos from one room to another if you are in your eighth month of pregnancy, but I certainly feel that you should let your body be your guide. If you feel energetic and want to be active, by all means do so. Unless you are among the women who really do have health problems during pregnancy, I don't feel you should treat yourself as if you have contracted some sort of illness. Pregnancy is not an illness. Follow through with your obstetrician's or midwife's instructions and your own natural feelings.

An enormous amount of information is available to parents-to-be. My experience has been that most of what you will find has been written by people who are not at all qualified. They have no credentials other than being writers and journalists who have interviewed psychologists or pediatricians and now present themselves as self-styled experts.

I call most of what you get in these books "cookbook information." They are recipes for what you should or should not do. Raising a child involves more than following a recipe, however. You need information to help you understand the basic issues and then go about making up your own mind. You can then make decisions that fit your lifestyle and philosophy. Trust yourselves to do what is right for your child. The best parents are confident parents.

In selecting books about child rearing, check the qualifications of the professionals. They should include extensive experience working with *parents* and *children*, not just people who have worked with psychiatric problems. I think it very important that the people who transmit information to you have experience with the everyday questions of parenthood as well as a good scientific background.

Does the advice you get from the professionals you talk to match your instinctive reaction? If you have a health problem during your pregnancy or immediately afterwards, you should discuss it with your obstetrician. For questions about the physical health of your child, consult your pediatrician. When it comes to psychological problems concerning child rearing, it is best to get your advice from people whose primary training is in the field of psychological development and parenthood.

Too much of the information you get from professionals is what I call "anti-parent." It is contrary to your natural inclinations and observations. When you hear your baby cry, for example, it is perfectly normal that you feel so anxious that you will want to jump up and pick up your baby and make her happy, no matter what she may need. Chances are someone will object with, "You don't want to spoil your baby, do you?" or "You don't want her to grow up to be dependent and cry every time she needs something, do you?"

The answer to both questions is obviously no. There is no relationship between making your baby happy and having her grow up to be spoiled, demanding, and dependent. In all likelihood, your feelings are not only correct, but they should be respected. Interfering with them is wrong.

Other people, including colleagues of mine, may tell you that babies sometimes cry for no reason at all. How could they possibly know this? After all, babies don't tell us why they cry. I would prefer to say that all babies cry for reasons,

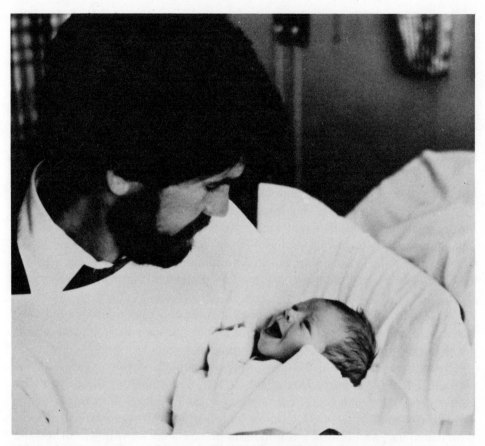

although we may not understand what they are. Or they may insist that "crying is good for the lungs." Such a statement is as ridiculous as saying that bleeding is good for the veins.

Parents generally notice that when they pick their baby up and put her to the breast or give her a bottle, she opens her eyes and makes direct eye-to-eye contact. She does this with whichever parent is feeding her. When I mention this to new parents, they smile knowingly, having experienced this lovely moment themselves. However, they are often told by doctors and nurses that, "Your baby can't see until she is three or four weeks old." Here is a perfect example of misinformation that is in direct contradiction to parents' own observations. Again, trust your own judgment. Your baby is responsive; she can see, she can hear, she can taste, she is learning. Even in her earliest days she is sensitive to what is going on around her and her behavior is complex. She is not the vegetable some people would like you to believe she is. Parents who realize that they are important in their babies' lives enjoy parenthood more and are more inclined to fulfill their babies' needs.

One mother I met told me her relatives were giving her as a gift the services of a baby nurse for two weeks. She felt uncomfortable with the idea but did not know why. In discussing it with me, she realized that she felt that in some indirect way they were saying, "You aren't good enough to take care of your child. You need an expert."

You will find, should you accept such a gift, that the baby nurse can easily become a wedge between you and your infant. "Have you washed your hands?" she will ask you sweetly as you reach out to take your child. Or as the father hurries in at the end of the day to see his baby, he may be told to stand back and wait until his body warms up so that the baby doesn't catch cold. You can never pay someone to be as good a caretaker of your child as you are. No one else will have the dedication, the feelings of love and protection that you have for your child.

People may say things that make you anxious and uncomfortable but their statements are often totally incorrect. Stop and question their information to check it against your own instincts and emotions.

The same is true of your feelings during pregnancy and your questions about yourself. For this reason be careful to select an obstetrician in whom you have confidence. You want a warm, considerate, "askable" person, someone to whom you can talk without feeling inferior or foolish. So many questions will crop up from day to day, and I think it is important to have a doctor with whom you feel comfortable.

You should be able to ask your doctor about such things as prepared (natural) childbirth, the use of drugs during delivery, and any other questions on your mind such as: Will he put you completely to sleep or use a local anesthetic? How does he feel about the father being present in the labor and delivery rooms? By the way, I think it's an excellent idea for fathers to meet with the obstetrician so that they can have their questions answered as well as the mothers'. Make your decision based not only on the obstetrician's responses but his emotional reactions to whatever preferences both of you have.

Once you have selected your obstetrician, you have in effect selected the hospital where the delivery will take place because of your doctor's connection with it. Find out as much as you can about the procedures the hospital follows in delivery and newborn baby care. If your obstetrician or the hospital does not look kindly upon having fathers present in the delivery room and this is something about which you feel strongly, you should by all means make sure your feelings and wishes are respected at the beginning of the pregnancy. If your doctor does not give you the support you want, this is the time to find a new one.

I believe that the period immediately after the baby is born is an extremely important time for you to begin to establish a bond with her. Some hospitals have a standard nursery from which the baby is removed and given to the mother only at feeding time. A mother who wants to spend more time with her infant may not be permitted to do so. Another alternative to explore and which I recommend is rooming-in. This arrangement allows the mother to spend most or all of her time with the baby from just after birth until they are discharged from the hospital. This is a good time to get to know your baby and for her to get to know you. Parents who have rooming-in always seem more confident than those who have little contact with their babies during the hospital stay.

Sometimes hospital regulations interfere with your urge to be with your child. When your baby cries, the nurse or doctor may discourage you from picking him up and comforting him. New mothers seem to have an inborn tendency, a very strong desire, to be close to their babies. It is almost as if they are driven to be responsive.

If you were to go for a walk in the forest and come upon a little bear cub, you would not want to get too close to it in case its parents were not far away. By touching the cub or doing anything to get between him and his parents, you would run the risk of being injured or even being killed. We respect this protective feeling in nature and do not consider the father or mother bear's feelings to be neurotic or inappropriate. Yet we tend to downgrade that same protective instinct in the care of human young. Your emotions have evolved over the course of time and have helped the species survive. If you were the kind of person who did not feel anxious when your baby cried or angry with a nurse for interfering with your natural impulses, I would worry about that.

In selecting the doctor and hospital, find out what the hospital's visiting hours are. All too many parents find it very frustrating if, after the baby is born, the father cannot be alone with his wife and infant. Many hospitals do have special hours for the father when other visitors are not allowed to be present. This gives parents an opportunity to be alone together with their baby, for both of them to hold their child and begin to form the family unit.

Some hospitals allow brothers and sisters to visit their mother and new sibling.

I think this is a marvelous idea and should be a universal procedure. Children need to see for themselves that their mother is happy and healthy and to see what the baby is like. Realizing that their mother has not forgotten them minimizes their feelings of abandonment. They have the opportunity to share in this joyous occasion. Young children are usually fascinated by a newborn infant, and such visits tend to reduce the degree of rivalry they may be feeling. If we can respect the integrity of the family at this critical early time, we can strengthen the bonds that family members share.

The question is often put to me as to whether or not I believe in natural childbirth. All childbirth, as far as I am concerned, is natural. The misconception that people have had is that natural childbirth is the equivalent of delivery without any medication or anesthetic.

I prefer to use the term "prepared childbirth," meaning that both husband and wife have been educated about what they are going to experience, usually through a course where all the stages of labor and delivery are discussed. The classes that are usually offered for parents on prepared childbirth should be attended by fathers as well as mothers so that both are equally familiar with what will take place.

Parents-to-be learn exercises that are performed prior to delivery, as well as breathing techniques to be practiced prior to and utilized during the various phases of delivery. The husband assists by participating in doing the exercises and breathing with his wife, and by offering encouragement and support throughout the process. By following the procedures, many women require very little if any medication.

Throughout history mothers delivered babies without an anesthetic. With improvements in medical technology, however, doctors believed that it would be advantageous to have mothers put to sleep during delivery. Many of them said that the mother served no purpose in the delivery, thereby depriving women of their natural instinct to participate in childbirth.

Based on my experience in talking with mothers who were conscious at the moment of birth, I believe couples should give very serious consideration to prepared childbirth. They have described it as a very exhilarating experience and have emphasized that there was something very emotional at that time which drew them closer together to their husbands. One mother I spoke to at the hospital with which I am associated said that she and her husband shared what she described as the most intense spiritual experience by being together at the moment their child came into this world.

I do believe that fathers should be encouraged to be in the labor and delivery rooms in order to have the chance to be close to their wives during this momentous event in life. I don't think they should be excluded and I feel that most wives would appreciate having their husbands present at that time. Every effort should be made to maintain that close tie that wife and husband have when a baby is born.

By having classes in prepared childbirth, you are not eliminating the possibility of being given medication. Should the pain become severe, you can certainly decide to ask for something to relieve it. Prepared childbirth is in no way synonomous with great pain. You may decide upon prepared childbirth and then find during delivery that you would like a painkiller to be administered. Don't let this take away from your pleasure or cause you to feel like a failure. The safe delivery of your baby and your health are far more important than making the use of medication a personal challenge.

Some women are terrified at the thought of any pain and feel anxious throughout their pregnancy. It is perfectly reasonable for you to wonder about the amount of pain and discomfort you will have. I think you should plan the birth of your child so that both of you will be as comfortable as possible.

Being born is a tough job. Babies as well as mothers work hard during the birth process. The sudden transition from a dark, constantly warm environment where the mother's heartbeat masks all other sounds to a world where there are raucous noises, changing temperatures, and bright lights is a shocking one.

One method which seeks to lessen this trauma and which is gaining slow but steady acceptance has been advocated by Dr. Frederick LeBoyer. He suggests that delivery take place in a room where the lights have been dimmed. Those attending the delivery speak softly, and the baby is placed in warm water even before the umbilical cord is cut. The transition from the womb to the outer world thus takes place more gradually than usual. Dr. LeBoyer's technique has been criticized by some as childbirth by candlelight and praised by others as a method where the effort is made to minimize the trauma for the baby by lessening the noise and warming the room temperature in the delivery room. I am in favor of his philosophy because it shows such respect for the needs of the baby and certainly think it is well worth considering and discussing with your obstetrician.

I encourage mothers and fathers to take classes together so that they both become familiar with labor, delivery, and the needs of the newborn infant. Most of the classes that are offered focus on the physical aspects of childbirth with pictures and diagrams of the baby and the various stages of pregnancy. It is also im-

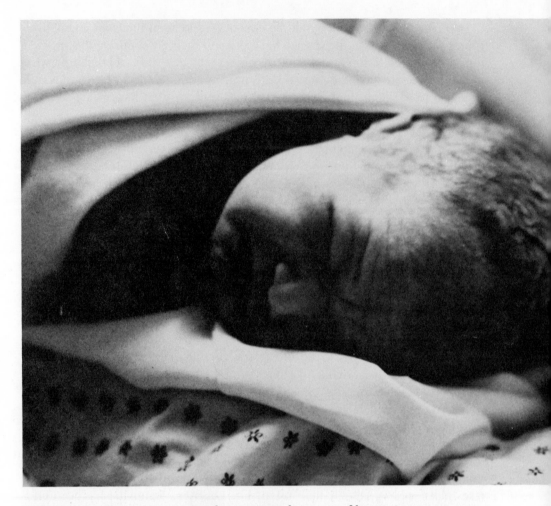

portant to pay some attention to the emotional aspects of becoming a parent, so that you can realize that you are not alone in your mixed feelings about parenthood. Everyone else in the class experiences feelings of anxiety and tension at some time during pregnancy.

I want to emphasize again how much in favor I am of fathers participating in the labor and delivery. There is tremendous excitement and drama in seeing a mother's joy as she hears the baby's first cry and for the father in holding his baby and feeling that he has been a part of the experience. Fathers with whom I've discussed the delivery of their child often become so excited that it is difficult for them to be coherent. A father will often describe it as if it were his pregnancy. He will talk about "our labor" and "our delivery."

Couples who have shared this experience seem so much closer as a result of having gone through it together. They seem universally to feel that this has been a very momentous occasion in their lives.

The reason I believe so strongly in prepared childbirth is because, as with child rearing in general, the more you are prepared, the better you are able to cope with all the contingencies that arise. The more you understand, the better prepared you are for dealing with the unexpected.

I think the ultimate in creativity is parenthood. All of us wish we could create life. Indeed, scientists are hard at work in laboratories trying to discover the secret of producing a new life. A woman can create life with her own body and I am convinced that men envy women that ability. Perhaps that's why men will use an

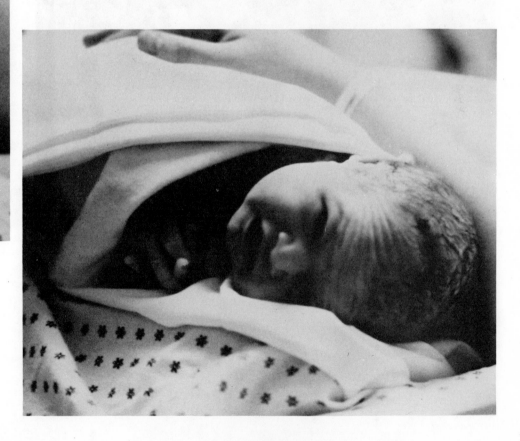

expression like "I have a pregnant idea" or "That's my baby!" Certainly the relationship between a man and a woman is solidified when they share in the birth experience and in the raising of their child.

When you bring up a child in whom you have instilled a sense of individuality and self-esteem, you are helping her grow toward emotional security. You will be making a tremendous investment in your child's early days, weeks, months—but you will get an enormous return on that investment.

LIFE WITH YOUR NEWBORN INFANT

As you walk into your home with your newborn infant, you will suddenly realize that you are facing a totally new experience—parenthood. You will have prepared yourself by reading, observing other parents, and seeking answers to your questions from your obstetrician, pediatrician, the nurses in the maternity ward, and the other professionals with whom you have had contact. Now you will be responsible for the care and welfare of your baby and, understandably, you may feel overwhelmed by the task.

You have probably given a considerable amount of thought to what your life will be like after the birth of your child. You are wise to plan ahead and give some thought to how you will cope with the new responsibilities and demands that will be made on your time. Let me caution you, however, about the need for flexibility. No matter how well thought out your arrangements are, your baby's particular needs and demands may force you to revise many of your plans. Despite your best intentions, you cannot possibly have anticipated the changes she will bring to your daily routines.

It's important for you to remember that you should try to make your baby's needs come first. Try to be well organized, but don't be too concerned if you

simply cannot accomplish everything you set out to do. Parenthood is very demanding, time-consuming, and also one of the most rewarding experiences you will be involved in. The baby's demands on your time and energy are well worth the efforts.

It is not uncommon for some mothers to suffer extreme mood changes during the days and weeks after delivery. You may feel unusually irritable or anxious. You may find yourself crying, sometimes for no reason at all. If you feel hemmed in and overwhelmed, as if a black cloud has descended and you have lost your desire to act, you may be suffering from what we call postpartum depression. This is caused by a combination of hormonal changes and the new pressures in your life. No matter how badly you may have wanted your baby or how excited you were about her arrival, you now have to juggle many new responsibilities. Both parents may begin to feel the stress caused by not feeling your physical best and having to face each day with far less sleep than you are used to getting.

As you may know, for some women pregnancy is a time when their moods vary greatly from one extreme to the other. Other women find themselves in an almost constant state of happiness. Whatever the reaction is, these moods are caused by slow but noticeable changes in the hormones. After delivery, other hormonal changes occur but this time more suddenly. The physiological changes that a mother undergoes cannot help but influence her emotional reactions. Changes in hormonal levels may cause a woman to question why she ever decided to have a child, to want to throw up her hands in despair and run away, to lash out at her husband. Although they are not experiencing the hormonal changes, fathers may find themselves behaving similarly. I think this is especially true of men who have been deeply involved in their wives' pregnancies and labors and are now participating actively in caring for their infants.

Be assured that your parental instincts, nature's way of ensuring the survival of the species, will help you get past this period. The warmth you feel when your baby is satisfied and looks happily into your eyes will carry you through these first few weeks or early months when you sometimes feel frustrated and despondent.

In extreme cases some mothers don't even want to touch their babies. They feel as if they cannot fight their negative emotions alone. If this happens to you, you should definitely seek professional help to overcome your depression.

For most parents, however, the postpartum blues will pass. I recommend strongly that, instead of suppressing your emotions and then feeling guilty about your frustrations with the baby, you talk to your spouse or sympathetic friends and relatives about what you are going through. Your moods are neither uncommon nor abnormal, and in all likelihood will pass.

Throughout your years as a parent you will find that you will often have moments when you feel anger and even hatred toward the child you actually love very much. Children sometimes get under your skin or fray your nerves. It is important for parents to understand this. If you can recognize that you have these feelings, you can contend with them far better than if you try to repress them.

The most universal comment I hear from new parents, and mothers in particular, is, "I never imagined how exhausted I would be." You suddenly have another human being making constant demands of you, and this is not someone to whom you can say, "Get it yourself. I'm busy now."

Some mothers may fall into an unfortunate pattern of fatigue and anger. Exhausted, they become easily irritated by the baby's endless demands. The baby is sensitive to his mother's moods and inevitably senses her irritation. His reaction is likely to be increased tension and fretfulness which will, of course, further increase the demands he makes on her.

I think it is important to try to avoid this exhaustion/frustration cycle. I believe the best way to do so is for both the husband and wife to share the responsibilities. If you feel you will need additional assistance, you might consider hiring someone to do the housework or cooking so you can devote time to your baby and still have an opportunity to relax and be alone with your spouse.

Another important concern of new parents is how to find the right pediatrician. Don't wait until the last minute to choose one. Take time during the pregnancy to meet and talk to pediatricians until you find someone with whom you feel comfortable and of whom you can ask whatever questions you have.

More often than not a pediatrician is recommended by your obstetrician and usually they will be affiliated with the same hospital. If the hospital where you deliver has the kind of humanistic approach to childbirth that I recommend, it is likely to show respect for children as well.

Discuss the pediatrician's philosophy with him or her. As a psychologist, I am interested in pediatricians who are psychologically oriented, but I urge parents to avoid one who is so concerned with emotional problems that he or she ignores your baby's physical needs. You and your baby will benefit from a pediatrician who is well trained, has a natural ability to make a child feel at ease, respects you as a person, and respects the individuality of your child.

All too often in my new parent classes I have talked to parents whose confidence in their abilities to care for their infant has been undermined by a well-meaning but opinionated baby nurse or so-called "experienced" relative. Remember—you are the best possible person to take care of your child.

There are some baby nurses who are narrow-minded about what newborn babies are like. They will tell you that infants are not capable of being responsive to you or their surroundings. This is totally incorrect. Babies need what we psychologists call sensory stimulation. I much prefer the word "cuddling" because when you pick your baby up and hug her, you are providing exactly this kind of stimulation. As you hold or gently bounce her, you exercise her muscles and she has a chance to see and hear what is going on around her.

A baby who has a chance to inspect the world around her while held in her parent's arms tends to feel happy and loved. Don't hesitate to cuddle your baby when she cries despite what people may say about spoiling her.

No one else, no matter how experienced or well trained, is likely to have the same protective feelings that result from the biological bond that links you to your baby. The sooner you begin to care for your baby, the stronger that bond will be and the greater your confidence in your ability to do a good job. You may

indeed feel nervous at first, but that is only natural. After all, parenting is somewhat new to you. You have, however, inherited certain natural drives and reflex actions—the same that we observe in other mammals. They are a part of your protective concern for your child.

These inborn reflex actions are part of what links you to your offspring. Scientists have observed that when a baby lamb is taken away from its mother just after birth even for only an hour, the mother lamb evidently loses her ability to recognize her baby. If, however, the mother is given a chance to nuzzle and lick her young, she will then be able to pick out her "baby" even in the midst of a large flock.

I have observed and spoken to hundreds of mothers and fathers of newborns, and it is my feeling that these protective instincts that animals show are shared by humans as well. Parents and babies show a need for closeness and stimulation. You will have a powerful urge to hold your baby, cuddle her, smile at her, talk to her, and play with her. Express these urges. Your baby may smile back at you, showing what seems to be happiness with you. Such exchanges are essential to your baby's healthy development of self-esteem and trust in you.

When your baby cries out and you respond to her, she develops a sense of trust in you. You can assume that your baby's cries mean she is unhappy because certain of her needs are not being met. Gratifying those needs helps her understand that human beings can be relied upon to help her feel comfortable.

Your baby may be crying because he is hungry and also has a need to suck. The mother who chooses to breast-feed will notice that nature has arranged for a very beautiful interplay between a baby's needs and yours—at the same time your baby becomes uncomfortable because he is hungry, you will usually feel discomfort as your breasts become engorged with milk. In response to your child's cries, you may automatically reach out and pick him up. As you hold him close to your body, he moves in the direction of your touch. This movement is the "rooting response" that babies have for the first four to six months of life. During this period babies move toward the touch when stroked on the face near the mouth. They begin to suck on the nearest object, in this case a nipple.

Babies very often cry because they are bored. Newborns need stimulation the way any other human being does. Since they are obviously incapable of picking up a magazine or walking over to the window to see what's happening outside, it is absolutely essential that you be sensitive to their need for stimulation or for some change in their environment. The important thing to remember is that your baby is telling you he is unhappy. Rather than letting him "cry it out," pick

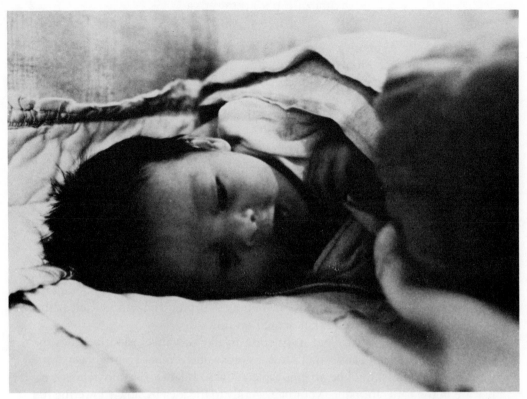

him up and hold him. This serves to increase his area of vision and at the same time he enjoys the sensation of closeness and being touched by you.

Some people, including well-meaning friends, may tell you that newborn babies cannot see. This is not at all true. They can see. You will probably notice that when you pick up your infant and put her to your breast or feed her a bottle, she will open her eyes and focus directly into yours. Why else would your baby look straight into your eyes unless she could, in fact, see? Why doesn't she look at your nose or your chin? Keep in mind that babies are much more responsive to you and how you are relating to them than most people give them credit for. This responsiveness will probably make you feel wonderful and is very important to your baby.

We know through scientific research that even just after birth babies tend to show a preference for looking at faces and bull's-eye-like patterns over horizontal lines, checkerboard patterns, or bright colors that are not patterned. So we know that a baby is capable of seeing and seems to have an inborn tendency to focus her eyes directly into those of the parent while she is being fed.

Babies are also responsive to sounds. They can smell and taste, and they have probably become accustomed to the rhythm of their mother's walk through the course of the pregnancy. Babies often enjoy being rocked gently. They seem to find it soothing and relaxing. This is probably because the baby felt these very same sensations even in the mother's womb before birth when he was protected and all his needs were automatically met.

Everyone loves to have his or her back rubbed and scratched, and babies are no exception. They get great pleasure from the stimulation of being touched and gently massaged. This kind of attention is part of the loving and caressing that babies need so much of, and which you will find yourself so eager to offer.

Bathing your infant can be a wonderful experience for both of you. Remember to test the water to make sure it's at a comfortable temperature. Use a small enough tub. Some parents are inclined to give a baby a bath at the same time each day. I don't think there's any reason to assume that it makes a difference when you bathe him, nor does he have to be bathed every day. Sometimes a sink is the best place to bathe the baby so long as you prop him up and clear the counter of anything that could fall or spill on him.

You can usually get excellent instruction in the best and easiest methods for bathing at the prenatal classes that most hospitals offer. What I particularly want to stress is that this should be an enjoyable activity. Infants generally relax when they are in the bath. Introduce your baby gently to the idea by slowly lowering his feet into the water. Be careful to avoid getting soap in his eyes or else he will protest vehemently the next time you try to scrub his head. As he gets older, he will want to splash around a bit. Bath time is a marvelous opportunity for a baby to begin manipulating objects and to enjoy playing in the water. Incidentally, when he's a few months older you can let him know that although he cannot play with water at the dinner table because he'll spill it all over the floor, it's all right for him to do it in the bathtub. And taking a bath with your child is also something he may enjoy very much and can be a perfectly healthy family experience.

I think it's as important for fathers to bathe their babies as it is for them to diaper and feed them. In general I prefer that they learn how by attending classes at the hospital, rather than learning at home from their wives. I don't doubt that a mother would make a very good teacher, but I think that by encouraging men to come to such classes, we are showing that it is important for fathers to be involved in child care at every stage and in every aspect of their children's lives.

A question which many parents ask me is, "Where should my baby sleep?" If there is an empty room for the baby, it is a good idea to put her to sleep there

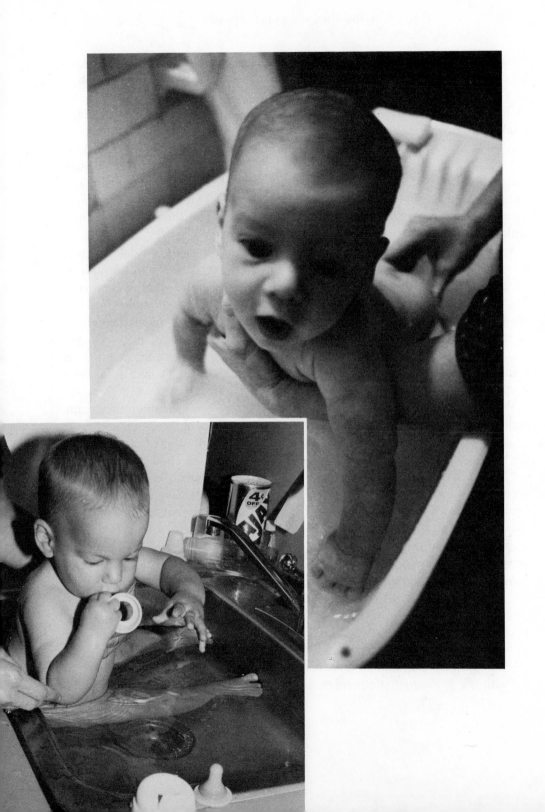

right from the start. At first you may find a carriage more convenient than a crib because it can be easily moved from one room to another, and its rocking motion may help your baby fall asleep.

Because parents need privacy I suggest that if possible the baby sleep in his own room. Some children become so used to sleeping in their parents' room that getting them to sleep in their own room later on may be very difficult. They need not feel the parents have to be right there beside them in order for them to be safe and secure. Granted that when the baby wakes up in the middle of the night, and babies do so well into the first year and sometimes even beyond, it is more convenient to have him right there. But I think it is important for both parents and children to have some privacy.

When your child is older you will probably want to teach him that a closed door is something that needs to be respected. Parents must be able to spend intimate moments together when the interruptions from children are minimized. This is especially true at a time when your relationship may be feeling some of the stresses of having a new infant. Sometimes parents begin to resent the child if he interferes too much with those tender moments that are important to a happy marriage. It is not uncommon for a father in particular to resent the fact that he is losing his wife to his child. However, not having an extra room for the baby doesn't mean your marriage will be destroyed.

What about having the baby share a room with an older sister or brother? I am inclined to tell parents to discuss the matter with the older child. You might want to ask him how he feels about the baby sharing his room, and where he thinks the baby should be. You may not want to deprive the older child of his privacy, but to him the baby's presence in your room may signify that you love his younger sibling more. You, of course, will make the final decision, but he will no doubt be pleased that you respect his feelings. Some children are delighted to share their room but may not understand that the baby will not be able to play with them right away. Prepare the older child in a realistic way, discussing the positive aspects as well as the problems.

More important than the question of where your baby sleeps and in what kind of bed is how tightly you wrap or swaddle him. I think that babies need to feel contact. They love when you hold and cuddle them. I have noticed in working with babies, and newborns in particular, that when they are tightly bundled, they seem to cry less than when they are left unwrapped.

Some people are afraid that by swaddling a baby in a blanket they are interfering with his movement. Remember that before a baby is born his body is surrounded by the fluid in his mother's uterus that kept him at an even temperature while all his needs were met. Being born involves quite a transition, and swaddling helps make it easier. Swaddling is comforting, a little like being cuddled or hugged.

It's important to recognize that infants are not as fragile as many people think. Some parents are almost afraid to touch their baby for fear that he will be injured. If you have ever watched a baby being born, you were probably impressed by how much pushing and pulling the baby underwent without coming apart or being damaged in any way. Babies just aren't as physically delicate as people tend to believe.

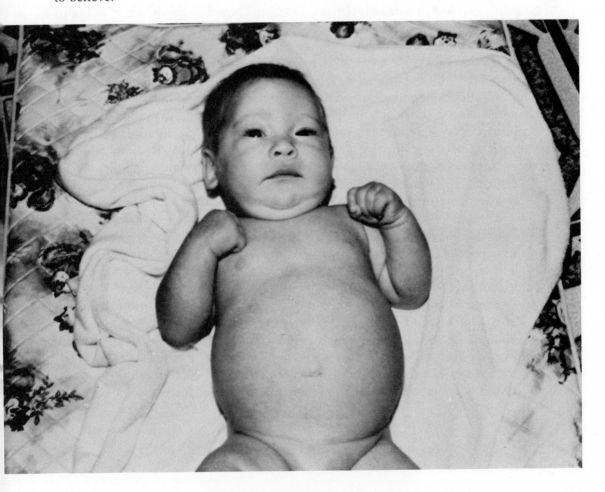

You may be surprised to find that your baby will wake up many times during the night. You will find yourself getting out of bed several times each night in response to your baby's cries. Almost all babies do this, no matter what your friends may tell you, and it is simply something you have to bear with until she sleeps through the night. In all likelihood she is hungry, but there are times when she simply needs to be held and comforted. If both parents are sharing the work load, it will be that much easier to get through this very frustrating but inevitable period in the baby's development.

Both parents need time to be alone with the baby and to be together to have the opportunity to begin to feel like a family. Don't hesitate to set limits on visits from even close friends and relatives. Let them know they are welcome, but only when you are ready to invite them.

You may suddenly find an enormous amount of strain on your marriage. You are both probably very tired and nervous about whether you are doing the right things for your newborn baby. Your familiar schedules and patterns have been forever altered. A working wife has to adjust to different demands. A husband for whom a neat house or apartment and quiet dinner hour meant the end of a difficult day at work must get used to having his priorities take second place to the baby's. Mealtime will probably depend entirely on your baby's feeding schedule.

A wife and husband who have had compatible ideas may now find themselves very much at odds over the care of their child. The husband may be jealous, consciously or unconsciously, of the huge amount of attention his wife is giving the baby, and the reverse is also often true. The wife may be resentful if she feels her husband is not involved enough with their child. Unresolved emotional conflicts about one's own parents may surface now that decisions have to be made about parenting. If you discuss these issues as openly and as often as they arise, chances are you will minimize possible friction.

As your baby grows day by day, so will your confidence in your innate understanding of what his needs are and how you can best satisfy them. The more responsive he becomes, the more caught up you will be in trying to understand the world through his eyes. As you conquer each new problem, your relief and excitement about the birth of a healthy infant will deepen into love for your baby—who looks to you to make the world a pleasurable place.

3

CHOOSING TO
BREAST-FEED
OR BOTTLE-FEED

PARENTS EVENTUALLY HAVE TO DECIDE whether to breast-feed or bottle-feed their baby. Give this question ample consideration well before the birth of your child. Don't wait until after delivery when a doctor may catch you at an unprepared moment and influence you against breast-feeding, as has been the case all too often in the past. Since breast-feeding involves the mother's time and physical presence, the decision should be primarily hers, but it certainly should be made after open discussion with the father.

As with every other stage in your pregnancy and parenthood, you will find that people will be quick to give you advice about how to feed your baby. Someone is sure to tell you that breast-feeding is unnatural, that it will make you feel like an animal, that your baby probably won't be able to get enough milk from your breasts, that you will be tied down too much.

I am convinced that those people envy you and that no matter what you are doing, they will be quick to point out that you are doing it incorrectly. Don't let such comments undermine your self-confidence or influence your decision.

Talk to women who have breast-fed their children or consult the La Leche League, a marvelous international organization established by women to offer other women encouragement and information about breast-feeding. Get the information, weigh the advantages and disadvantages against your particular needs, and then make the choice.

Most mothers have two fundamental questions they want resolved: Will I produce enough milk to satisfy my baby's nutritional needs? Will I sacrifice my independence by being tied to the baby's feeding schedule?

I can assure you that except under unusual circumstances your milk supply will be more than sufficient to fulfill your baby's needs. In fact, the more you

breast-feed, the more milk you produce. Babies actually take in most of the milk they need and empty the mother's breast during the first three to five minutes of a feeding. At this point, if you check to see whether you still have milk and discover that very little is coming out, don't be concerned. Your child has gotten the milk she needs. She will nevertheless continue to suck because doing so gives her great pleasure and is an inborn need that must be satisfied.

My answer to the second question is yes, breast-feeding does tie a mother down to the demands of her baby. This is precisely what nature meant to happen. A happy, content baby is one who has as much positive contact with his parents as possible. Breast-feeding guarantees that the mother spends a great deal of time holding and cuddling her infant.

Because breast-feeding so beautifully and naturally satisfies the physical and emotional needs of mother and child, I suggest that you strongly consider doing it. I hasten to add that I have no doubt that you can raise a happy, healthy baby that is fed from a bottle. Should you choose that alternative, you need not feel as if you are depriving your baby of a crucial aspect of his development. If there is no compelling health or other reason why you should not breast-feed and you are having trouble deciding, I urge you to breast-feed.

The feeding relationship between you and your baby is a very important one and should be pleasant and gratifying. Babies tend to cry not only because they have hunger pangs, but also because of their need for sucking satisfaction. Some babies are born with calluses on their thumbs which seems to indicate that they were sucking even before birth.

Nature has arranged it so that a baby's need to suck becomes more intense at the same time that he needs food. The nursing mother generally becomes physically uncomfortable when her breasts are engorged with milk around the time that her baby begins to cry—a signal that he is uncomfortable due to hunger pains.

When you instinctively reach out to pick up your infant because his cries create anxiety in you and you hold him close to your body, you are automatically gratifying yet another one of his very strong needs—to be cuddled and given the close physical contact essential to his emotional development. In fact, I suggest to mothers who are bottle-feeding that they hold their babies when they feed them rather than propping the bottle on a pillow or using a bottle holder.

Your warmth and touch are as important to your infant as the sound of your voice, your smile, and even your smell. I am convinced that odor is an important part of a baby's getting to know his parents. In our culture we tend to mask smells

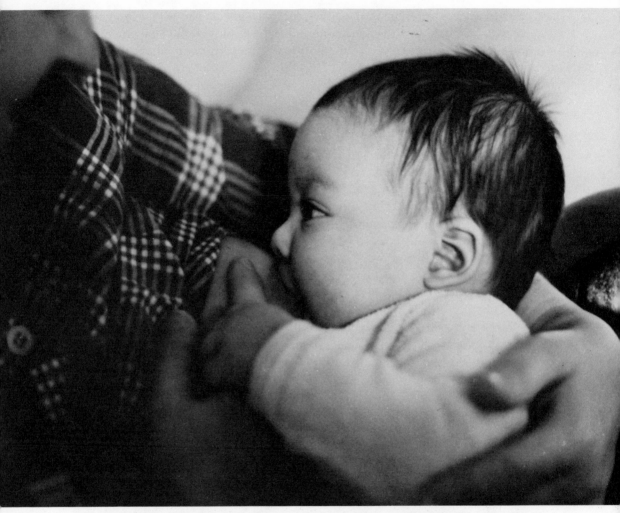

with perfumes and deodorants, whereas in the animal world the sense of smell is an important part of species identification. I believe that odor plays an important role in the bonding that takes place between parents and their children.

Right from birth to about five months of age you will notice that if you stroke your baby's face or touch his lip he will move in the direction of that touch. This is called the rooting response and it helps him find what he needs to take away the pangs of hunger and satisfy his sucking need. As his mouth fastens upon your nipple, his hunger and need to suck are gratified and the tension in your breasts is relieved as they are emptied. Not only does this provide you with relaxation and enjoyment, but your pleasure is communicated to him by the look on your face and the tone of your voice. Your calm, happy mood further enhances his sense of well-being.

Another result of breast-feeding is that when the baby begins to suck, the mother will feel contractions in her uterus. These contractions are nature's way of helping a woman's body return to its prepregnancy condition.

Your baby will continue to suck even after he has had his fill of milk and until his sucking need is gratified to the point where he can relax. As I mentioned earlier, the breast will probably be empty by now so that the baby can properly satisfy his sucking need without having to take in more milk than he needs. A bottle-fed baby, on the other hand, drinks the same quantity of milk throughout the feeding and he may continue to suck even after he has taken in enough to satisfy his appetite. You can solve this problem by giving him nipples with smaller holes so that he has to work harder in an effort to satisfy his urge to suck.

Your baby will let you know when he is ready to release your breast or the bottle. His muscles relax, his head drops to the side, and he will resemble a rag doll as he peacefully drifts into sleep.

Very often there is a lovely moment in this sequence when the baby tightens his facial muscles to break the suction and remove himself from your breast. It looks as if he is smiling and I believe that he is smiling. All too many doctors will insist that it is not a smile but an expression on a baby's face caused by gas pains. I find this idea totally absurd. Gas has never produced a smile in me or in anybody else I know.

The fact of the matter is that he is now satisfied and is breaking the suction to release himself from the nipple. After all, when people, even very young children, are happy and gratified, they smile. Unhappy, frustrated people tend to purse their lips, as if they are still hanging on to something because they are reluctant to let go when their needs haven't been satisfied. When you smile back, as you inevitably will, you are expressing your enjoyment of the moment. I believe that this exchange is the basis for the social smile later on.

Sometimes a baby will be cranky and fretful even after she has emptied her bottle. Perhaps after one or two sucks on a second bottle, she suddenly relaxes and indicates that she has had enough. Remember, it is as important that her sucking need be met as that she get enough food.

Another advantage of breast-feeding is that a mother's milk is healthier for a baby than cows' milk or formula. Allergies to human milk rarely occur while

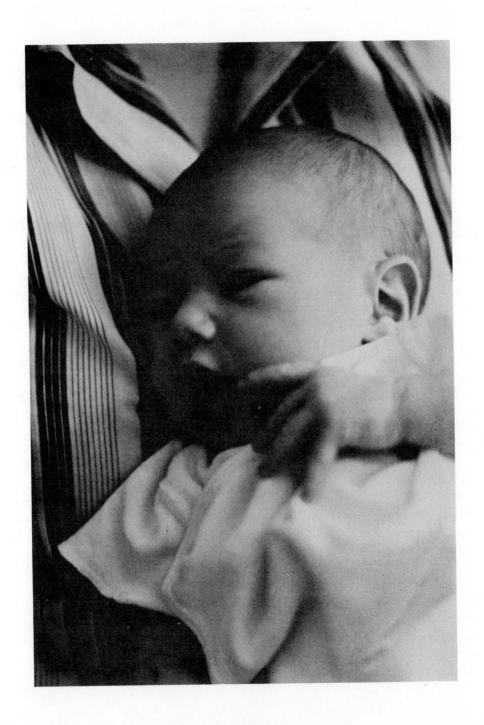

allergies to cows' milk are not uncommon. Human milk is understandably more geared to human physiology than is cows' milk. What could be more logical than for nature to have endowed mothers with the ability to provide their children with the kind of nutrients they require?

Mothers' milk also passes on to their babies the mothers' immunities against diseases for the first six to twelve months of life. Antibodies, the chemicals in the body that cause immunity, are present in the milk. If you are not fanatic about sterility and your baby has normal exposure to household germs, as your immunities are transmitted to him he builds up a stronger resistance to germs in a kind of booster reaction.

Babies sometimes spit up quite a bit after they are fed. The odor of a breast-fed baby's spit is never sour. Bottle-fed babies frequently have a sour smell because cows' milk or formula tends to curdle.

Some mothers-to-be anticipate that breast-feeding will be a burden. Yes, you do have to be there, but I believe that nature has arranged things in just this way so that you will be there to offer your love, to cuddle, and to play with your baby. In fact, I use the length of time between feedings as a model for the number of hours you can be away from your baby, whether to go off to work, run errands, or spend some time by yourself. Keep in mind, too, that by breast-feeding you are sparing yourself the problem of carting around all sorts of equipment, such as bottles, formula, and nipples every time you and the baby leave the house. Breast-feeding mothers have the advantage of always carrying their equipment with them. Don't be embarrassed about breast-feeding in public. You can do it without exposing yourself. Ask the nurse in the hospital to show you how. It is a perfectly natural function, and certainly societal attitudes are changing so that a baby at her mother's breast is no longer considered shocking or obscene.

Breast-feeding should not be viewed as an all-or-nothing proposition. If you decide you are not comfortable with the idea of breast-feeding or for some reason you cannot do so, don't feel guilty or worry about short-changing your child. A mother who is reluctant to breast-feed—but does so because of peer pressure or a desire to do what is best for her baby despite her true inclinations—is likely to approach feedings with tension and anxiety.

It is much more important for you to feel relaxed and secure when you feed your child than how you feed him. Babies grow up to be happy, healthy, productive adults as long as they are not ignored and receive the amount of love and nurturing they require as children, whether they are breast-fed or bottle-fed.

I do encourage parents to give a bottle from time to time even when they are

breast-feeding. Some breast-feeding enthusiasts may disagree on the grounds that this tends to weaken the bond breast-feeding creates between the mother and infant, and because of the nutritional advantages of mothers' milk. There are times, however, when a mother may be away from her baby at feeding time. By giving him an occasional bottle, you are preparing your infant for the times you will be unable to breast-feed him. If you are determined that your baby drink only your milk, you can express your milk into the bottle before you leave.

I suggest that when you begin to accustom your baby to taking a bottle, the mother should offer it to him at times other than when she is about to be absent from the home. Babies learn far more quickly and accurately than most people would believe, and they may resist taking a bottle if they associate it with separation from their mother.

The occasional bottle also affords fathers a chance to participate in feeding their babies. I have spoken with many fathers who are envious of the fact that they cannot feed their infants. They see the enormous pleasure their wives derive from gratifying their child's needs and, quite understandably, they want to be able to share in this enjoyment. I think it is important for fathers to be very much involved in every aspect of parenthood, and feeding an infant is certainly one of which he should not be deprived. Once the baby gets used to taking the bottle from the mother, the father should begin to give it to him while the mother is present. Later on the father or anyone else can offer the bottle.

Eventually the baby should become accustomed to the idea. Don't be shocked, however, if your baby absolutely rejects the bottle. He knows a good thing when he has it! Babies frequently wean themselves from the breast spontaneously. My own son gave up breast-feeding when he was ten months old but still wanted to have a bottle at naptime or bedtime.

My feeling is that some flexibility is important so that you can feel free to be away from time to time. Otherwise there may come a point when you are feeling so tied down to your baby's demands that you may feel resentment toward him.

Parents often ask me how I feel about pacifiers. In general, I would prefer that you avoid using them. If the child needs to suck, the sucking should accompany the feeling of something going into the stomach. Babies need to be picked up and cuddled. I find that parents who use a pacifier plug it into the baby's mouth instead and this deprives the child of your holding and cuddling. A pacifier is not a suitable substitute for your love and attention.

I've seen babies become extremely attached to pacifiers even after their need for sucking has been met. In a sense a pacifier may cause the baby to continue sucking beyond the time when she would otherwise have outgrown this need.

There are circumstances for which I would make an exception, for example when a baby is hospitalized or ill or suffering in some way, such as when he is teething. If for some reason you cannot comfort him or alleviate whatever is causing him pain, the pacifier may give him the extra measure of reassurance for which he is crying out.

I believe the most appropriate time for oral needs to be satisifed is during infancy, and certainly would not push a baby into being weaned too early for fear that these needs may then be prolonged into childhood. A lot of doctors will tell you that a child should be weaned when his teeth come through. Unless you find that breast-feeding becomes uncomfortable for you at this point, I would recommend that you continue at least into the second year so that his need for sucking can be adequately met.

Some mothers find that their children begin to cling more than usual when they try to wean them. When weaning your child from the breast or bottle, you can avoid an abrupt transition by having gotten her used to a cup when she was perhaps four or five months of age. Although she won't be able to hold the cup herself and most of the liquid will drip down her face, she will at least become familiar with the concept. I prefer real cups to those that are enclosed at the top with an opening for a straw.

Most children find it easier to give up the bottle during the day than at night. Going off to sleep is like regressing to an earlier stage of development. Sucking on the bottle at bedtime makes it easier for the baby to return to that infantile state.

When you finally wean your child, in all likelihood he will be fussing more because he is reluctant to surrender the breast or bottle even at bedtime. It helps to spend some extra time holding him and singing or reading to him, so that he is able to relax enough to fall asleep. In general, an extra bit of cuddling will help your baby through this sometimes difficult transition.

While I am delighted that more and more mothers are choosing to breast-feed and that the World Health Organization as well as the American Academy of Pediatrics now encourage it, I want to reemphasize that the more important point is for your baby to get as much cuddling and love as you can offer.

Many parents worry that if they satisfy their baby's needs he will want to stay a baby for the rest of his life. This is simply not true. A satisfied baby is eager to progress and explore all the stages of development. As long as you hold him, talk to him, or sing to him while he is being fed and whenever else he needs to be cuddled, you will be providing the closeness and stimulation so crucial to his emotional and physical health.

4

YOUR BABY'S EMOTIONAL NEEDS

SOME YEARS AGO I conducted a survey of new mothers at the hospital with which I am affiliated. I asked them to list the questions which concerned them most as mothers of newborn infants. The one that appeared most frequently at the top of the list was, "How can I avoid spoiling my baby?" My answer to this question is very simple. You cannot spoil a newborn baby.

Babies during most of the first year of life are helpless and very dependent. They don't know how to satisfy their own needs. If parents don't help them, they cry a lot and eventually learn to give up easily. They also feel unloved and neglected, and they lose trust in people. I am sure you don't want your baby to feel this way. By responding to your baby and making him happy, you help him develop trust in people.

The fear that most parents have of spoiling their child is based on the fact that they have a very strong desire to satisfy the baby's needs. Nature has arranged it so that parents experience very intense feelings of distress when they hear their baby crying or see that their child is uncomfortable. The impulse to rush over and relieve the baby's unhappiness is a healthy one. Unfortunately, we live in a society that believes that satisfying a child's needs is the equivalent of weakening

him, that frustration somehow leads to strength. Hence, the all too common anxiety that responding to a baby means having him grow up to be a whining, dependent adult.

When dependency needs have been met in infancy, those needs go away, much the same way that hunger subsides when you have eaten. If these infantile dependency needs are frustrated or not met during this time of life, they persist and lead to whining and dependent behavior in later childhood and even into adult life. A child whose parents did not provide satisfaction of her needs during infancy and childhood may be more apt to try to gain attention through destructive means. I do not mean to imply that not meeting your baby's needs once in a while or occasionally leaving her in the care of someone you trust will cause your child to grow up to be a juvenile delinquent. What I am talking about is allowing yourself to respond to your baby's demands for recognition as often and wholeheartedly as you are naturally inclined to do.

Parents want to make their babies happy but they have been led to believe that being nice to their children will turn them into demanding brats. This is absolutely not so. Strength comes more from having been satisfied than it does from constant frustration.

Your baby is totally dependent on you for his survival. His only way to let you know he needs something is by crying. He may be hungry or need to suck, he may feel pain or cold or be wet. He may be bored, which is as frustrating a condition for infants as it is for adults.

Your baby is dependent on you—and this is precisely as it should be. Dependence is the foundation on which to build his independence.

Children who have never had the opportunity to become dependent on one person for any significant period of time have problems developing independence. Independence is a developmental skill that comes from learning how to extricate oneself from dependency.

A child's first year of life is the time when she should be developing a sense of trust in the world and good feelings about herself as a human being. We believe that when babies are first born they do not see themselves as entities separate from their parents. Their perception of the universe is that when they feel something, their mother or father also feels it.

At some point during this early period, the infant must undergo a process referred to as individuation. The baby begins to understand that something else is out there, other than himself. This understanding comes about when he cries and you respond. If he calls out and nothing happens, he will have a harder time developing a sense of individuality and will be inclined to withdraw by going off to sleep.

As he acquires a sense of selfhood, he is also learning that he is important to you. If he were not, why would you bother responding to him? Feeling important leads to a strong sense of self-esteem, which is an important element in human development and mental health. Adults who have a sense of self-esteem and feel they can deal with life without being easily overwhelmed, who like themselves, do so because when they were young they had parents who were responsive to their needs. This is why I say don't be afraid that you are spoiling your child by being loving and kind, and by making him happy. By giving him the feeling that he is a central figure in your life, you are reducing any tendencies to be destructive or self-destructive when he is older.

One of the worst bits of advice you are likely to hear from both professionals and friends when your baby cries is, "Let the baby cry it out." This is precisely what you should not do. By ignoring her cries, not only are you communicating the message that she is not important to you, but you are teaching her that she cannot rely upon those around her for help.

Believing that if you satisfy your baby's needs she will remain a baby forever is as absurd as telling a hungry person not to eat or she will continue eating until she bursts. People who are hungry are preoccupied with food. Eating makes their hunger go away and frees them from their preoccupation with food. The same applies to infantile dependency needs. The best way to make them disappear is to satisfy them.

If you consistently ignore your baby's cries at bedtime, if you turn off the light and close her door, she will scream and scream in anger and panic until she eventually gives up and falls asleep. This may be of immediate benefit to you, but the long-range effect may be that she will have learned to tune out the world and will give up easily and withdraw into sleep when faced with a stressful condition or a challenge.

However, when your baby is nine or ten months old and decides she wants you to play with her at two in the morning, I definitely do not think you should indulge her wish. She is old enough to learn that this is not the time to socialize.

Once you have assured yourself that nothing is hurting her, show her that you are annoyed with her behavior. Put her back down in the crib. If she gets up again, put her down again repeatedly. Let her know that you are not there to play. If you let her cry without responding to her, she may fear she has been abandoned. Children have terrible fears of being abandoned and if you fail to respond that fear is realized. In other words, it is important for you to respond to her, but the response does not have to be positive. It can be annoyance or mild anger.

Some children really are frightened and have nightmares. They may be startled by a noise in the night. Leaving a light on often comforts them. Whatever you can do to help alleviate your child's anxiety is fine.

Babies not only need responsive parents, they also need what psychologists refer to as sensory stimulation but I prefer to call cuddling. Your baby will cry when he has a specific need or is distressed. If he is hungry and needs to suck, you can solve his problem by giving him your breast or a bottle. At other times, however, the reason for his unhappiness is not so clear-cut, but what he may be telling you is, "I'm bored. I need to be held. I need to look around me from the safety of your arms instead of from my crib."

But, you may ask, if I keep responding to my infant and picking him up when he cries, won't he want even more cuddling and attention? Yes, most likely he will, because he will have discovered how satisfying and pleasurable it is to be with you. This is the basis for good communication and a positive relationship for years to come. This is precisely one of the important elements in a healthy parent-child relationship.

Nurturing your baby means satisfying not just his physical needs but his emotional needs as well. Babies are not vegetables—they are born with all their senses functioning and they have the capacity to learn. They need diversion as well as warmth and loving and look to you to provide them with these things.

When you hold your baby in your arms and move around, you are opening up to her a wider, more visually interesting world—faces, colors, different-textured objects. Babies love various sounds and are even temporarily fascinated sometimes by the sound of a vacuum cleaner or an air conditioner. They love to be touched and stroked and cuddled in your arms in an easy, relaxed way.

Their need for cuddling and other forms of sensory stimulation is probably related to their environment before birth. In the womb (uterus) the fetus is kept warm and protected by the liquid that surrounds it. It is exposed to the sound of its mother's heartbeat and to its mother's movements. Thus, after the baby is born he may be comforted by those same stimuli he experienced when he was in that peaceful environment without abrupt sounds and changes in temperature, and he was automatically fed.

Babies usually tend to enjoy new and novel situations but may feel more secure if their parents are holding them when they are exposed to such situations.

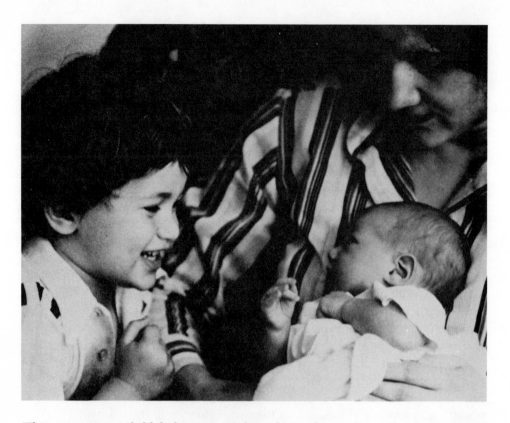

This means your child feels secure in his relationship with you, and you should respect this feeling. He will look around a lot more at strangers if he is in your arms. If he is held by someone with whom he is unfamiliar, he may quickly start to cry and reach out for you. Your baby loves you and feels secure with you. This does not suggest that your baby will grow up to be a clinging child. He reacts this way now because he is indeed a baby and turns to you for protection. Later on he will become more adventurous if he is not overly frightened now.

In the middle months of his first year your baby may become sufficiently comfortable about the world to go to strangers quite willingly, but may revert from time to time to his earlier pattern and want to stay close to you again.

When you first come home with your new baby you may want no one else holding him. People may tease or criticize you about this and may accuse you of being overprotective. But there is nothing wrong with following your feelings. You have every right to follow your own protective urges.

Babies need to establish a strong attachment to their parents. This is why I encourage parents to have a great deal of physical contact with the baby in the first hours and days of the baby's life. Don't hesitate to hold him, stay close to him, and take him with you when you go places.

When babies begin to crawl, they usually want to stay in an area where they are close enough to keep an eye on you. Your baby may suddenly begin to cry if he doesn't see you right there. He becomes very frightened because he is afraid of being abandoned.

As your baby grows and develops, you will find that his curiosity about other people and his surroundings also increases. A marvelous chain reaction takes place. The more love and stimulation a baby receives and the more confident he feels that you will be there for him, the more likely he is to want to explore his environment. The wider the range of his emotional and physical explorations, the greater the resources he has to draw upon as he ventures further and further into the world.

Babies learn by imitating their parents. We have discovered that babies begin to imitate their parents' facial expressions at a very early age. They enjoy watching their mothers and fathers and doing things in the same way. This imitative behavior is the basis for many informal games parents play with children. "How big are you?" a parent will ask his baby, raising his hands in the air and indicating, "So big!" And the baby will gleefully raise her own hands high in the air in response to her father's playful attention.

Many of the skills the baby develops during her first year of life are based on learning through imitation. When you introduce your child to solid food, you may illustrate how to swallow it by opening your mouth and swallowing a spoonful. As you teach her how to drink from a cup, you put the cup to your lips and take a sip.

When you smile at your child and she smiles back, when you say hello, wave good-bye or blow her a kiss, you are teaching her the basics of social behavior. I think it's an excellent idea for a baby to be present at the dinner table, perhaps in an infant seat or a high chair. It gives her a chance to see what you are doing and you will find that not long into the first year your baby will want to do what you are doing, to use a spoon and a cup and have a plate in front of her. Joining you at meals and watching you eat also gives her a sense of family—a feeling of participation. It is also an excellent opportunity for her to learn how people interact with one another and to try new things. Your baby watches and listens to you.

You will find that with each new skill your baby acquires he will gain greater

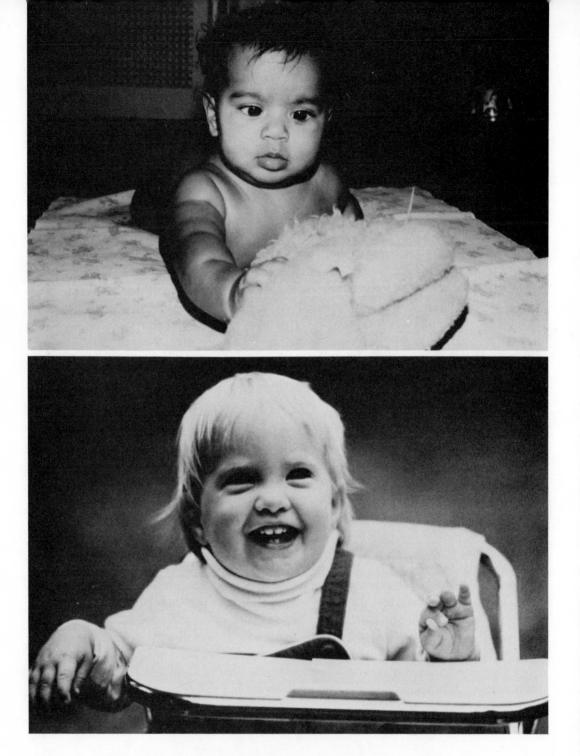

confidence in himself and will become more and more motivated to explore his world. You cannot simply turn your back on him. As he becomes more adventurous, he will check your reactions to what he does. Your approval teaches him that he is permitted exploration and gives him the courage to try something perhaps even more exciting. At the same time, your disapproval will help him avoid doing things that could be harmful or unacceptable. He will usually test your responses to see whether you are consistent.

Try to be consistent in your responses. It will help him understand you and the world better. The first time your baby accidentally pours his juice over his head, you might find it cute and react in an amused fashion. Noting your smile, he may repeat his action, looking to see whether he gets the same reaction. If you now show disapproval rather than amusement, it can be extremely confusing and

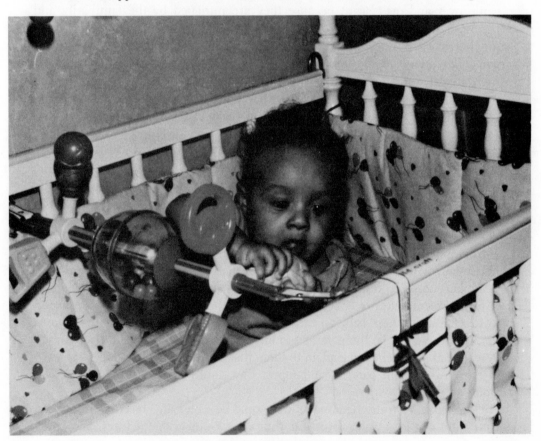

cause him to repeat spilling his juice in an attempt to determine how you really do feel about this new activity.

Even when your disapproval is apparent from the outset, he may seem to be testing you by repeating his action. His smile of delight may convince you that he is "out to get you." What is actually taking place is this: He has discovered that he can produce in you a certain response, and, like any careful laboratory scientist, he is experimenting to determine whether the response will recur a second and third time under the same circumstances. His smile signifies that he is excited about his ability to cause things to happen and to figure out how. This kind of experimentation helps him learn about life and people and is of positive value even though it presents you with constant challenges.

Another way that babies learn is by playing with toys. Babies can play the same game over and over again because they are intrigued by the familiarity and predictability. I believe that parents should let a child play with a particular toy as much as she wants even if it is repetitive play. You will find, too, that your child will frequently want the same story read several nights in a row. You may be more than ready to go on to a new book, but your baby seems to demand the same book she has heard for the last three nights. Once she has gotten used to something and is really familiar with it, she may want to go on to something new.

Although a child under a year old may not understand what you are reading, you should nevertheless read to her. Your child will enjoy the familiar ritual— the sound of your voice and hearing the same words. She begins to anticipate sounds and words and eventually she may begin to try to imitate the sounds you make while she pretends she is reading the book herself.

I am totally opposed to programmed learning for babies and to the idea of parents setting up a schedule or curriculum. Even if you are a teacher by profession, remember, your main responsibility to your baby is not that of education—instead you should be responsive, loving, tender, and caring with your baby.

Education should not be forced on a baby. I have known parents who put up word charts on their baby's bedroom wall. When the baby eventually pronounced these words, the parents proudly declared that their child had learned how to read. I have had to explain to them that all their child had done was learn to recognize certain patterns and repeat the sounds his father or mother said aloud to him.

Don't push learning. Reading aloud should be a pleasant, relaxing time when your child can look up at you, hear your voice, look at the pictures, and enjoy

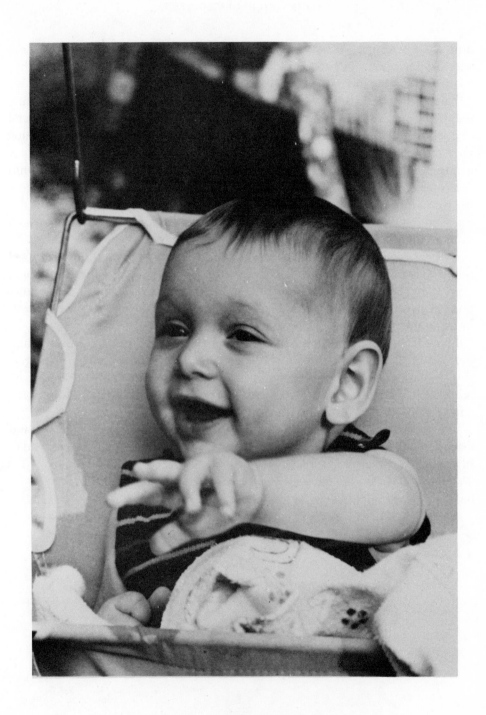

time alone with you. If he begins to pick up certain words and associate them with the appropriate pictures, fine, but don't turn the experience into a stressful, instructional situation.

Parents often tell me they have problems putting their children to bed because they resist sleep and cry and fuss at bedtime. After questioning them further I frequently find that their baby was not ready for sleep. If you insist upon putting your baby to bed at your convenience rather than when she is sleepy, you may wind up with a child who fights sleep and keeps you busy comforting her until she is ready. Help your child make the transition from wakefulness to the sleeping world by singing to her, reading to her, and rocking her. If the end of the day is a soothing, pleasant period that you share with your baby, she will look forward to those moments with you and fall asleep with much less fussing.

Being a good parent means spending a lot of time with your child. I know of one pediatrician who often tells parents that the best parent is the happy one, even if the parent's happiness means constantly turning the child over to someone else to be cared for. As far as I am concerned, this is taking the role of parenthood far too lightly.

I have known children whose parents were reluctant to give them the attention they required and thus created a very regrettable situation. A child who badgers you constantly and is ignored becomes a whiner. By not paying attention until he becomes so irritating that you are forced to respond, you have taught him a pattern of behavior that is hard to unlearn.

Older children often tell me, "I think that parents should pay attention and listen to what their children say. I think parents sometimes listen but think you're silly and that makes you feel bad."

When you respond to the cries of your baby and listen to what your older child has to tell you, you are being a responsive parent.

5

AS YOUR BABY'S WORLD CHANGES

UP UNTIL NOW I have been mostly addressing myself to the needs, problems, and behavior of young infants. As demanding and time-consuming as new babies can be, you will reach the point in your child's first year when you will realize that taking care of a very young infant may have been easier than caring for a crawling baby.

The day will come when you find that with each new skill there are a whole new series of problems that you must cope with, and you will have to adapt your behavior to the changing needs of your child.

Children are individuals. They each develop at their individual pace and with highly individual temperaments. Although there is a normal range within which certain skills develop, it really makes no difference at all whether your child develops at the early or late end of that range. This is why I hesitate to give parents a timetable for the growth and development of their child. Whether a baby walks at the age of ten months or fourteen months is not important. He or she is developing within the normal range. The baby who begins to walk at ten months is not necessarily more intelligent than the one who walks at fourteen months.

Parents should not push their children to do things before they are ready.

While they need challenges, pushing them beyond their abilities can cause them to avoid challenges and therefore interfere with learning. Parents of young children frequently compare their children to other children to see who is smarter or perhaps faster. Such comparisons frequently cause parental anxiety and are of no value whatsoever to the child. Don't let yourself get drawn into comparisons or be upset because your neighbor says her child sleeps through the night when yours does not. Every parent feels their child is the only one who wakes up while all others are sleeping. The chances are that your neighbor's child wakes up as often as yours but that she is not telling you the truth. Your most important concern should be that your baby is happy and that you are meeting her needs.

The transitions of the first year are largely based upon a child's developmental skills. The day your baby begins to move from one place to another on her own

your life will undergo a radical change. You have to clear the poisons out from under the sink and put away anything that might be dangerous to her health. As she begins to pull herself up to a standing position, you may want to clear some of the knickknacks off your coffee table and watch her carefully when she is in the kitchen near the stove. You will have to begin to institute rules and regulations, a subject which is discussed in greater detail in a later chapter concerning discipline.

As babies' skills increase, so do their frustrations. They reach a point where they want to undertake certain things they are not yet capable of handling. They may decide that they want to do exactly what their mother or father is doing. Reading a book or newspaper can become next to impossible if your baby makes up his mind that he wants to read too. He may bang his hands on the page glee-fully or tear the newspaper out from under you. He enjoys this, but it can be very frustrating to you.

There is not much you can do about his attempt to involve himself in your activities except to try and find something you think he may enjoy more. At times he will be happy to accept his own book as a replacement, but frequently he wants only your book or your newspaper. Nothing else will do. You might try giving him a section of the newspaper you have already read and don't mind hav-ing torn to shreds. I have seen one-year-old children sitting contentedly on the floor, examining the paper, and babbling cheerfully as if they were reading. They were probably imitating their parents reading aloud. Moments like these make the joy of parenthood worth all the frustrations and sleepless nights you have been through.

Children often do the same sort of thing with their favorite picture books. Hav-ing watched and enjoyed their parents read to them, they will sit quietly and turn

the pages, pretending to read aloud. By the way, studies seem to indicate that children who are read to when they are young show a strong interest in books and read more as they get older. If they experience books as a way of the world opening up to them, they will turn to books for stimulation and gratification, and as a source of information when they want to learn about something.

You may discover that during the middle to end of your child's first year she will begin to imitate your actions more and more. The toy telephone you bought is likely to gather dust because your baby wants no part of it. She is only interested in using the real telephone just like her mother and father do. She may delight in playing with the pots and pans as she watches you cook. Many of the objects in your cupboards or closets make wonderful toys. A child can be absolutely fascinated by a cardboard carton that she can turn upside down and push around the house or she may enjoy sitting inside it, creating her own cozy environment. Aluminum foil can entertain a child for hours—crumple it up and it is shiny and makes interesting sounds, or wrap it around a hanger and you have a glittery mobile. Pots and pans turn into drums or hats and make strange sounds when she babbles into them.

You will discover that when your baby gets to be about nine or ten months of age, she will giggle and squeal with delight if you conceal an object she is interested in and then suddenly "find" it. As her imagination develops, this kind of game becomes a real favorite. Playing peekaboo with you will amuse her from time to time as she alternates between feeling just a little bit apprehensive as you vanish and then happily reassured when you reappear.

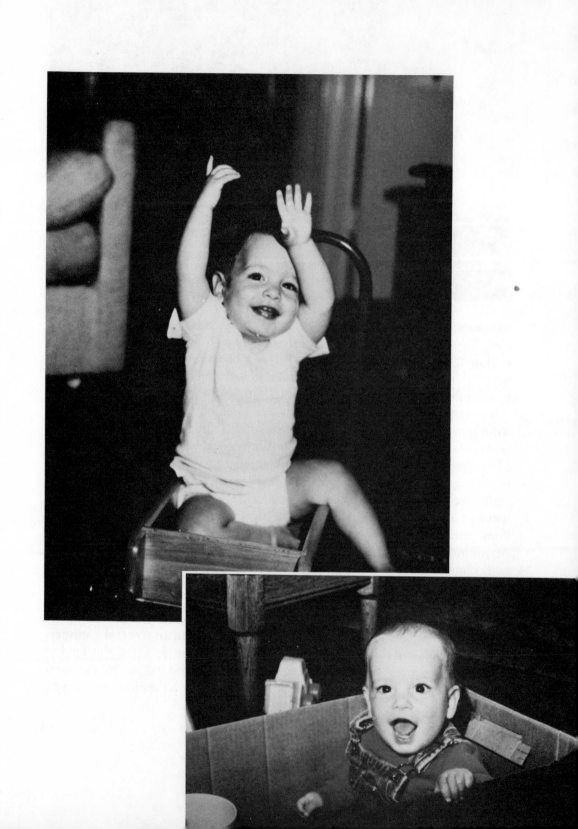

Meals can be more difficult and certainly messier as she insists on having her own spoon to eat with and rejects your feeding her. She may be more tempted to bang it up and down on the table than in eating with it. This kind of curiosity is healthy and should be encouraged. However, you cannot let it go on and on without some limits. Although it will be difficult, try to get her to use the spoon to feed herself by putting the food on the spoon and letting her hold it as you guide it to her mouth. This is easier said than done, but may turn out to be more fascinating to her in the long run than banging the spoon.

You will find that your child may sometimes want to touch or smear her food. I think it's fair to let her do so in order to satisfy her curiosity. If you try to prevent this, you will only be intensifying the need and feeding eventually will turn into a war of nerves. Mealtime should be enjoyable and as free from tension as possible. Certainly children eat better and are more responsive to food if their earliest experiences with food are positive.

This can be a very frustrating period in that your baby will have discovered that when he releases something, it can cause things to happen. I have seen children who, when they release an object, look up as well as down to see where it has gone. You will probably spend a lot of time picking up spoons and toys as your baby experiments with releasing things while learning about gravity. It is precisely this sort of play that helps children understand one aspect of how the world works.

At this stage babies have not yet learned that dropping a glass of milk is any different from dropping one of their wooden blocks. Your child will be astonished to discover that letting go of his cup can change the color of the floor, make a puddle, cause you to bend down and begin to wipe up the liquid, and perhaps show anger or annoyance. What a wonderful experience this is for a child—with a mere release of his hand, he can cause so many things to happen.

Needless to say, this is so fascinating to him that he will probably want to do it again to determine whether the same sequence of events will occur. This kind of experimentation may be tedious for you, and you may feel he is out to make your life miserable, but he is not. He simply wants to experiment and learn. The more time you spend with him helping him establish some understanding of the world, the more fascinated and curious he will be. At the same time you can use these opportunities to teach him what is acceptable and what is not. Children who are not permitted to try new things or who get little response may lose their motivation and excitement about learning how the world works. As trying as it will be at times, you have to respond in order to encourage positive behavior and learning.

Your response and encouragement are also the basic elements in establishing the idea of discipline, the rules and regulations that govern behavior. If a parent, instead of channeling the child's curiosity toward an acceptable way of dropping things, screams or hits the child for spilling his milk, the child will have learned nothing other than that his parent became frightening for some unknown reason.

This is hardly the message you want to communicate to your baby. Far better to hand him another cup of milk and, as he looks you straight in the eye as if to let you know that he is about to spill it again, you can say no, very firmly but without frightening him. Replace the cup with something that he can drop, a piece of crumpled paper or a plastic toy, for example, and show him by dropping it yourself while smiling and then giving it to him. He will realize that dropping some things is permissible, while dropping his milk is not. At this age he may not

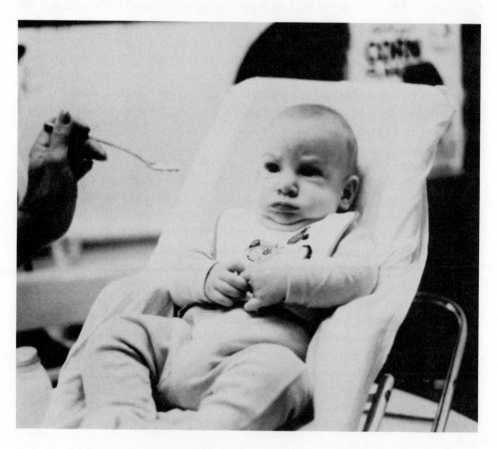

yet understand why this is so, but if you do not stifle his curiosity, the understanding will come in time.

Babies are not born knowing that certain things are acceptable and certain things are not. If they can learn the distinction within the context of a loving parental relationship, parents have a much greater influence on teaching their child what is acceptable and what is not. You are establishing rules and regulations which give your baby even greater freedom to do whatever she wants within the limits. This is the main ingredient of discipline. You must remember, however, that limits which are too confining will cause frustration and interfere with learning.

Sometime around the middle of the first year, babies begin to eat solid foods. This is a good time to give them a chance to taste all sorts of foods, before they have developed prejudices about beets or apples or whatever it happens to be. Prepare yourself for the possibility that your baby may develop a liking for unusual foods—perhaps even spinach. I recently saw a baby happily sucking away at a lemon while the adults around her winced at the sight. I see nothing wrong with having babies test new tastes, with the exception of certain extremely spicy foods that may be too difficult for them to digest.

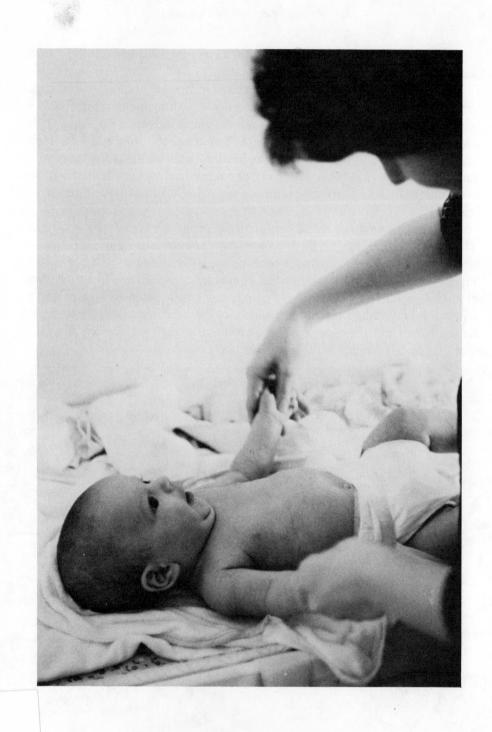

Around this time, as your baby becomes much more active, diapering her can become more of a problem. Many babies hate to be restricted and bounce around and protest when they are placed flat on their backs to be changed. The only solution to this is to change them as quickly as possible and get it over with. Fortunately, in this day of diapers with self-sealing flaps, you have an easier time of it than if you choose to deal with safety pins that can prick the baby as she wriggles around.

Parents often ask me when to wean their child. I believe that there really is no hard and fast rule to follow as far as weaning is concerned. I would caution you against weaning your baby before he is ready. During a baby's first year of life, he should be developing a sense of trust in his parents. This is best accomplished when his parents are responsive to his needs. The need for sucking satisfaction is an important one. Don't try to wean your baby in his first year. Wait until he is over a year old and begin slowly, while you are teaching him to feed himself. Some babies can be weaned from the breast or bottle when they are close to a year old, but most babies require a bottle until they are three and, in some instances, even older. Trying to wean your child before he is ready will intensify his need for sucking gratification.

Toilet training is one process which has no place in a child's first year. A child is not physically ready for toilet training until she is approximately eighteen months of age. Prior to this she has neither the emotional capacity nor the muscular control to cope with being toilet trained. Toilet training before the child is ready can be an extremely traumatic experience for her.

During the second half of the first year of life, when your child is able to move from place to place, grasp objects and release them, he is ready to learn what he can do in relation to what he cannot. In other words, when he attempts to do something that is dangerous or destructive, tell him "no" and remove him from the situation. Make sure he understands that you disapprove but that you are not angry with him for having tried it out.

If he is expressing his curiosity in a manner that is, for whatever reason, unacceptable to you, try to substitute another activity for the undesirable one so that the energy he is directing toward accomplishing something is not totally blocked. The moment you say no without an explanation or substitution, you are likely to be faced with a frustrated child and a potential temper tantrum. Since he is not yet old enough to know how to cope with frustration, the tantrum may be his only outlet. You can avoid this painful situation by offering acceptable diversions.

Children who are ignored until they get into trouble quickly learn to get recognition in negative ways. You avoid establishing such a pattern by giving your child attention when all is well, rather than waiting until something goes wrong. Some parents will pay no attention to their children's achievements in school until the day the child brings home a poor report card. Feeling neglected, he may have decided that failing was the only way to get any attention. By becoming more punitive, parents reinforce the pattern. This is why I encourage parents whose child is acting in a destructive or constantly aggressive manner to give him more time and attention rather than punish him with rejection, which would only make his behavior worse and perpetuate the negative pattern.

Children need to have some freedom of movement to explore. For this reason some children find a playpen too restrictive. When they are not only able but very eager to crawl around and investigate their surroundings, they can become frustrated by having their freedom of movement limited to such a small space. They are likely to spend most of their time inside the playpen, screaming to get out of it. While on the topic of freedom of movement, I want to emphasize my strong opposition to the use of a leash on a child. I think it is totally demeaning for a child to be on a leash. It is far preferable to have him sitting in a walker or stroller.

It is not only important for children to learn how to cope with limits and restrictions, it is also important for them to learn how to deal with freedom. In my thirty years of experience as a psychologist, I have found that more people who get into trouble do so because as children they were never given sufficient freedom under the guidance of a caring and loving adult who helped them make decisions and guided their choices.

6

DISCIPLINE
AND YOUR BABY

ALTHOUGH MOST PEOPLE use the words discipline and punishment interchangeably, I think it's important for parents to understand that these terms are completely different. Discipline refers to rules and regulations that are meant to protect against harm or destructiveness. Punishment is the price we pay for violating those rules and regulations. In my mind, discipline is an extension of your love for your child, a way to show him that you care by setting down rules that allow him to lead a safe and happy life without infringing upon the rights of others.

If no rules of behavior are established for a child—or if these rules are unclear—the child will probably be anxious and perhaps destructive, not out of hostility but because he is asking someone to set limits for him. Instituting discipline is a continuation of your love and concern for your baby. It shows that you care. Now that your baby is growing and interacting with the rest of the world, you need to learn how to help him cope with his curiosity about his environment. In this way he will be able to direct his interest outside himself so he will not function just in terms of his own impulses without regard for other people's feelings. By establishing rules for your child, you will have equipped him with the ability to deal with many of the situations that occur in life.

A child is most effectively disciplined by those in whom he has a sense of trust, those who have offered him protection and who have satisfied his needs. When a child knows that his parents love him, he has a strong inclination to follow the rules in order to preserve that love. When you express your pleasure and pride in your child's behavior, you are reinforcing it. On the other hand, expressing annoyance, dissatisfaction, and rejection of his behavior makes it clear that you disapprove. In this way, you guide your child's behavior.

A child who has no limits usually becomes very anxious. I have treated adults whose parents set no limits or were inconsistent in enforcing rules and regulations. As a result, these patients had difficulty coping with their impulses and had trouble forming relationships. Having never learned the rules and regulations, they never learned how to express themselves with reasonable constraint. These people grew up to be either very destructive or terribly inhibited because they never learned how to deal with rules and could not control themselves. When the rules and regulations are clear-cut, however, children can investigate the unfamiliar without feeling overwhelmed by unknown limits.

If you are consistent in your expressions of approval and disapproval, you will be more effective in helping your child understand and accept rules and regulations.

In the first months of your baby's life, it is totally inappropriate to set rigid rules and regulations. Your child will not be able to understand and respond to them. Moreover, the baby's helplessness prevents her from harming herself or others. When she gets a little older, say five or six months, she will probably begin to experiment with more complex voluntary activities by reaching out for objects or throwing or dropping things.

During the second six months of the first year, babies reach an important step in their development. They begin to move about more on their own. This will undoubtedly make your life more complicated since you have to keep a more watchful eye on your baby to make sure he doesn't eat the laundry detergent or drink the water in the cat's bowl.

Parents often talk about "childproofing" their home, and I agree with this idea up to a point. As a child becomes more curious about her environment and more active in her exploration of it, you must remove all dangerous or irreplaceable objects. But if you take everything away, you are depriving your baby of her first opportunity to understand that not everything is permissible and that there are, in fact, rules and regulations that govern her life.

The electrical outlet is a very good example of what I have in mind. As your

child is crawling about your home she is likely to discover outlets and to put her finger in them to find out what will happen. Obviously this can be very danger-ous and something you don't want her to do. One alternative is to cover them up with some sort of plastic device, but this is unwise because there will be times when she is visiting in another home where the outlets are not covered. Another alternative, which I prefer and recommend, is that you help the child learn that you totally disapprove of her playing with outlets.

This can be accomplished by telling her "no" in a very firm tone of voice the first time she happens upon the electric outlet and puts her finger in it. Surprised by your manner, she may look at you, then at her finger as she wonders what she did to provoke this reaction. She may put her finger back in the outlet while looking at you to see if she will get the same response. Again you should say "no" in the same firm way.

It's a good idea to show her an outlet on the other side of the room, perhaps, or in another room. Most likely, she will try putting her fingers in that as well. She may try one hand and then the other, wondering if it is a particular hand you disapprove of. She may try every possible approach until she realizes that it does not matter which finger or hand—it is all outlets that are forbidden.

Remember, the point is not to frighten her, merely to convince her how seri-ous you are in your objections. Don't be surprised if, after the fourth or fifth time this sequence is repeated, your child smiles when you frown and say no. It's not that she is happy that you are upset or annoyed. The fact is that she has figured out the formula. She should not poke her fingers in the outlet. Her smile is one of understanding, rather than joy and satisfaction over your unhappiness.

Another point I would like to make about this example is that if you are too busy or impatient to stay with your child while she tests the alternatives and until your disapproval is firmly established in her mind, she is likely to conclude that it's all right to poke her finger in the outlet as long as you are not in the room. She comes away with the idea that there are certain things she can do in front of parents and certain things she can do behind their backs.

If Mommy is the one who has taught her about staying away from outlets, it's perfectly reasonable from the child's point of view to test out the situation with Daddy or Aunt Muriel or Uncle Richard. In other words, once the child has found out there are certain things that she cannot do, she wants to know whether this rule is consistent for all people. Teaching a baby the rules and regulations can be a trying process, but it is an important and necessary one.

Some parents have complained to me that when they follow my recommenda-

tion in this or similar situations, the child thinks this is a game. They worry that he isn't taking them seriously enough because he appears to be having a lot of fun. When you stop and think about it, however, games are made up of rules and regulations, and children do enjoy testing them out; this is another reason I am convinced that children want and like rules and regulations—discipline.

Given the chance to engage in any kind of activity, children usually decide to play a game. In fact, if you put a group of three- or four-year-olds together in one room with several objects and leave them alone for fifteen minutes, you will generally find that they have made up a game involving these objects and governed by definite rules.

Many parents ask me if I believe in punishment. It's not something I do or do not believe in. Punishment is a reality, the penalty for wrongdoing. What do you do when a child violates rules and regulations? You have to indicate your rejection of that behavior and some punishment is appropriate. It is very confusing to a child if you set rules and then do not enforce them. The question therefore is, what represents a good and fair punishment?

If your child feels your love and is concerned about your approval, you will be in a position to use your reactions as a reward or punishment for acceptable or unacceptable behavior. Your annoyance and dissatisfaction are a form of punishment. On the other hand, if you show pride and satisfaction in what she has done, you are, in a sense, rewarding her efforts.

I am totally opposed to material rewards, such as an extra dessert or a new toy. Nor should you deprive a child of dessert or a toy because she has been disobedient—this only intensifies her need for whatever has been taken away. A child who is sent to bed early often starts to feel that going to sleep even at the regular hour is a punishment. She may subsequently try to extend her bedtime, almost as if being allowed to stay up later proves she is loved that much more.

I think it is only fair that the form of punishment be in proportion to the crime. Research has shown that very severe punishment is far less effective than milder forms of punishment. Severe punishment causes a child to feel that the parent is mean and she will feel self-righteous rather than guilty for having violated a rule. It is also important for the punishment to be imposed at the time the rule is broken, not a week later when the child can no longer make the connection between cause and effect.

While this does not apply during the first year of life, I have found that bringing children, particularly older children, into the decision-making process works very well when you are trying to establish a method of punishment. You will generally find that when asked what a fair punishment would be, children are inclined to be far more severe than you are. I know of a five-year-old who, when asked to decide on a punishment, said, "Don't feed me for a month." By discussing the alternatives with your child until you come up with something that is appropriate, you are helping him develop a sense of right and wrong. If the form of punishment is too severe, the child may come away feeling that the next time he will have to be more careful not to get caught. It is far better for the child to realize he has done something wrong, to feel guilty, and to use his own inner controls in order to avoid getting involved in the situation again.

Do I believe in spanking children? Absolutely not, unless of course a child's life is in danger. If your child is climbing up on the windowsill on the fourth or fifth floor, I don't think that is the time to say to him, "Sweetheart, if you fall out that window you are going to hurt yourself." I would grab him and spank him in order to convey the idea that this is truly forbidden, even at the expense of frightening him. I would much rather have a slightly traumatized live child than a well-adjusted one lying badly injured on the sidewalk below. When it comes to life-threatening situations, parents have to act very quickly. There is no time to give a warning. Apologize afterwards about the spanking, but make him understand the dangers and that you never want him to do this again.

Many parents feel that by spanking a child they are teaching him violence. They are absolutely correct. There is no evidence whatsoever that shows spanking to be good for children. In fact, there are studies that show physical punishment to be psychologically very harmful. It undermines self-confidence, is humiliating, and leads to deep resentment, fear, and retaliation. While a spanking may cause your child to do what you want at the moment, the long-term disadvantages are too devastating to be worth it. Children learn violence by living in a family or society that condones violence.

I am also opposed to mothers who, when faced with having to punish a child, say, "Wait until your father comes home. I'm going to tell him what you did and he'll teach you how to behave." I think it is highly unfair to put the father in the position of being the one who is feared and whose role is primarily negative; furthermore, he should not have to deal with the consequences of an act in which he was not originally involved.

There comes a point in your baby's development when you have to help her learn to control her impulses, to direct her responses to more socially useful ends, to avoid being destructive. She may object to the rules but will nevertheless have to accept them. She will eventually understand that she will have a happier and easier relationship with you and the other people in her life if she follows the regulations. If you have given your child a sense of self-esteem, and she likes herself, she will be much more inclined to want to please others. The love and acceptance you have shown and your being there to respond to her make you all the more important as a person to be pleased. If you are available to meet her needs or if you are severely punitive, she will be much more inclined to disregard your wishes or actually rebel and be defiant of you.

7

COPING WITH YOUR OWN NEEDS

As FAR AS I AM CONCERNED no one can take better care of a child than her parents. You instinctively know how to love her and how to respond to her needs—this helps her develop into a trusting human being. The joy and pride you feel when you nurture her and watch her grow is communicated in many different ways to your child, who is so sensitive to your feelings. Your pleasure reinforces her pleasure, which is then transmitted back to you in a wonderful interplay of emotions. This is why I believe it is crucial, particularly in the first few years of her life, that you spend as much time as possible with your child so that she benefits to the fullest from your care.

I recognize, however, that parents do need to have some time away from their child, and it's important to consider how best to provide for your child's needs while still being able to gratify your own interests. Most people probably take for granted how free they actually are until they have children. The contrast between your life before and after the birth of a baby is enormous. There will be times when you may feel trapped by your obligations.

You may long for the days when you could go out to the movies without having to make any arrangements other than to decide which show to see. Drawbacks like this come with parenthood, and I certainly appreciate that the moment will come when you really do feel you must get out of the house, alone, away from your baby, no matter how much you love and enjoy her.

Your primary consideration should be your child's emotional health, and not simply doing what is more convenient for you. Babies are sensitive to what is happening around them and are particularly sensitive to whether or not you are present. After the age of two they have a better developed understanding of time and can differentiate between yesterday, today, and tomorrow.

A parent who is absent for perhaps days at a time may find that her baby suffers from severe separation anxiety or becomes so grief-stricken that she will actually show signs of fear and depression. During their first two years of life, babies find it very difficult to understand that when you have gone somewhere, you are in fact coming back. Very young babies simply cannot grasp this concept.

So it is difficult, if not impossible, to prepare a baby for your absence. This is why I recommend if possible that you avoid being away from your child for prolonged periods of time. I realize that emergencies do arise that make it necessary for you to be away for several days at a time. If at all possible, however, try to avoid or limit these separations. They can be terribly upsetting and cause a child to be fearful and anxious.

When you need someone to care for your baby, choose a caretaker or babysitter who is warm and loving and respectful toward you and your baby. He or she should make every effort to care for your baby according to your philosophy of child rearing. Your baby needs someone who is flexible, someone who can understand his feelings and see the world through his eyes. Choose someone who is herself a happy person, who enjoys children, and whose priority is playing with and cuddling children.

Generally speaking, your baby will like and get along with someone you like. Again, as in other areas of child rearing, trust your instincts. If your child lets you know that he is not comfortable with someone you have hired, no matter how highly recommended or well-qualified that person may be, respect his feelings. Sometimes a babysitter may appear to be perfectly pleasant while you are present, but treat your child in a less than desirable manner once you have left. If you have reason to believe that something may have happened in your absence to cause your baby to react negatively to the babysitter, I would be wary about using her again.

Give your baby a chance to get used to the person who will be taking care of him while you are still present to comfort and reassure him. Have the sitter come about an hour before you are scheduled to leave so that the baby can see you talking to her and understand that this is a person you trust. The opportunity to become familiar with a new babysitter in your presence will make your departure far less threatening. This also gives him an opportunity to get used to the fact that you will be leaving.

It is frightening to a baby when he awakes to find a stranger in his room and his parents gone. It can also cause him to try to avoid going to sleep. Therefore, don't make the mistake of putting a child to sleep before the babysitter arrives. Some parents assume that they are sparing their baby anxiety by not letting him know they are leaving. This solution often backfires.

Imagine a four-month-old child whose father has rocked him and sung to him and put him to sleep peacefully. The parents then go out for the evening, leaving him in the care of a sitter whom he has never seen before. The child awakens, hungry or perhaps simply wanting some cuddling. His means of communication is a cry of distress to let his parents know that he needs them. He quite reasonably expects his cries to produce his parents. This time, rather than having his father or mother appear to make him feel safe and comfortable, he is faced with a stranger.

As far as the baby is concerned, going to sleep has caused his parents to go away. The next time his father tries to put him to sleep by rocking and singing to him, he may understandably fight sleep out of fear that, by giving in to his exhaustion, he will cause his parents to disappear again.

I do feel that children can benefit from being away from parents for several hours and from spending time with other adults who are attuned to their needs. This helps a child learn that his parents do indeed go away from time to time, but that they also come back. However, I would advise against spending entire nights away from your baby during his first two years. Even an overnight absence can create anxiety that can cause sleep problems for him. If you are away repeatedly, he may develop serious fears about his ability to trust and depend on you.

Recently I met with a couple who had an eleven-month-old child. He was a marvelously happy little boy, playful and bouncy. They had felt it would be all right to leave him with a babysitter with whom the child was familiar so that they could take a week's vacation.

While they were gone, the child became fretful, cried at night, and showed signs of depression by refusing to eat. Feeling it would be upsetting for the parents to know that their child missed them so much, the babysitter did not tell them of the baby's unhappiness when they called periodically to see if there were any problems. Consequently, the child went through an agonizing seven days, reacting as if the parents were gone forever, never to return. In his inability to understand time, one week seemed like an eternity.

Upon the parents' return, they were devastated when their child turned away and ignored them. Resentful of their absence, he clung to the sitter and treated them with a kind of detachment. The parents, needless to say, were very concerned and unhappy about his behavior.

I explained to them that his reaction would probably subside in a matter of days but that they might find other problems developing. Having at first rejected the parents when they returned, the baby now would not let the mother out of his sight, screaming and crying whenever she left the room. He not only resisted going to sleep at night but, when he finally dropped off, he awoke many times during the night and was reassured only when the parents came into the room to demonstrate that they were still there and had not abandoned him again.

In reviewing the situation with me, the couple agreed that it would have been a far better solution for them and their child if they had taken the child and the babysitter with them. That way they would have had an opportunity to spend some time alone and yet be close enough to prevent the child's anxiety and feeling that he had been abandoned.

I realize that bringing another person along as a babysitter is an added expense. But the extra cost is probably worth it.

Although traveling even short distances with a baby does involve bringing with you all sorts of paraphernalia, particularly if you are bottle-feeding, I certainly

think it is an option well worth considering. Babies really can travel almost anywhere with you, and they gain considerably from the experience. A baby who is exposed to new people and places together with his parents achieves a very healthy curiosity about the world around him.

I know of parents who take their babies hiking, camping, to museums, and to restaurants. If you are comfortable there, the chances are good that your baby will be, too. After all, the pioneers took their children in covered wagons across rough terrain and into unfamiliar territory, and they survived quite well. An older child will probably make more demands, but the pleasure and excitement in sharing these special events with you is well worth it.

More and more parents want to know whether their baby will suffer if they continue to work after the baby is born. I cannot stress too highly the benefits children gain by having one responsive parent at home most of the time as the primary caretaker of the child. Having the parent there to satisfy a baby's needs is too important to be considered lightly.

If, however, both parents must work or choose to do so, I think it important that one of them try to spend perhaps two to three hours in the middle of the day at home with the child. A mother who arranges her work schedule so that she can breast-feed her baby at midday is able to maintain the close contact that is so essential to a baby's development and still handle her job.

I realize that what I am suggesting may be impractical—but I am addressing myself not to the convenience of the parent or even to his or her happiness, but to the optimal conditions for raising a happy and healthy baby. I am, of course, very aware that many mothers, especially single mothers, do not have the luxury of establishing their own schedules because of financial hardship. In this case, you must be especially careful in your choice of who takes care of your child, and make it very clear to that person that he or she is to abide by your decisions about how to raise the baby.

Recently I spoke to a woman who works at the same hospital as I do. She told me that she got enormous pleasure out of being with her baby, but she had to work because the family needed the money. She was considering working three full days and being at home the other four, taking care of her child. I suggested that she consider a more flexible schedule—working a five-hour day, five days a week. She could thus put in the same number of hours but, by spreading them out over a longer period of time, she would be able to get home in the middle of the day to be with her child.

For a parent who cannot get away from work this way, I sometimes suggest that

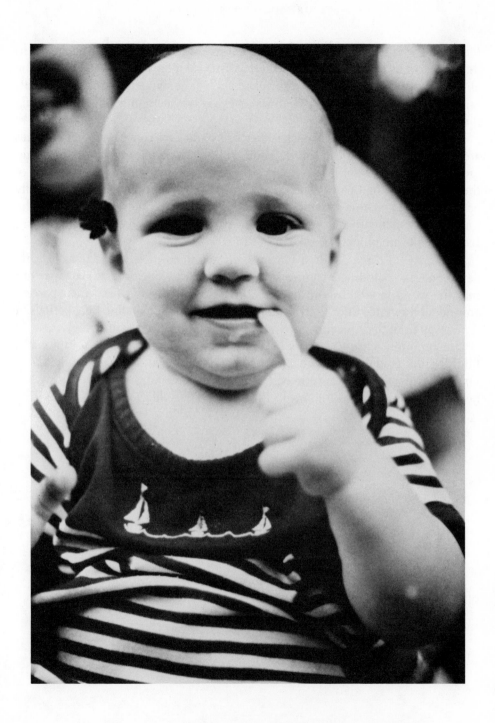

the person who cares for the child bring her to the place of work at lunchtime so that they can be together for a while at that time. Not only is this beneficial to the child because she does not have to spend the whole day apart from the parent, but parents who have to work find that they do not feel guilty about neglecting their child.

Some industries have set up what they call child care centers, so that facilities are available for taking care of the child while the parents are at work. I would prefer to see parents put in two hours during the course of the day, taking care of their children in that particular center. This arrangement provides the flexibility parents need to assume responsibility for their children. There is no limit to the long-range benefits society can gain from parent-child centers where children's requirements are properly met.

By the age of three children have usually mastered most of the tasks of early development, including weaning and toilet training. They are ready to go out into the world to establish greater independence and do not need their parents around all the time. Prior to that, children have trouble spending long periods of time away from their parents or in an organized educational setting.

Use common sense to strike a balance between maintaining your sanity and fulfilling the commitment you made when you decided to have a child. Your instincts will probably be your best guide to determining how to satisfy your needs without causing you to neglect those of your child.

8

HANDLING
SPECIAL PROBLEMS

PARENTS ARE NATURALLY PROTECTIVE toward their children. They want to do what is best for them so they will grow up to be emotionally healthy adults. Part of this protectiveness includes wanting to shield children from hurts and hazards.

When a baby gets a cold or runs a fever parents are usually worried, and understandably so. They want to relieve their child's distress and are nervous about the cold developing into something more serious. This is one reason why I stress how important it is that you feel comfortable calling your pediatrician for advice and reassurance. You should have a doctor who is respectful and gives responsible answers to your questions. This is as much a part of good medical treatment as regularly scheduled checkups for your child.

Pediatricians maintain a chart of the baby's height and weight to keep track of his physical development. His pattern of growth can be an indication of many potential problems, emotional as well as physical. An extreme example is a syndrome known as "failure to thrive," which sometimes occurs among babies who have not received sufficient cuddling and warmth and, as a result, stop growing. My main point, however, is that regular visits will help you feel confident that your baby is getting the medical attention he needs and that any possible problems will be diagnosed in time.

If you are uncomfortable and suspect that your pediatrician is not giving enough attention to your concerns, don't hesitate to go to another doctor to get his opinion. I respect the anxiety that parents have. In many instances I myself have diagnosed a serious problem that another doctor ignored simply because he felt he was dealing with an overanxious parent. Parental anxiety has to be dealt with. It is hard enough being a parent and having to cope with the normal day-to-day issues—why should you have to experience any additional anxiety?

There may be occasions when, despite your vigilance, an accident happens or your baby contracts an illness serious enough that she has to be hospitalized. There is very little you can do psychologically to prepare a child who is less than a year old for such a situation. But you should spend as much time as possible with her at the hospital, especially when she has to undergo any painful procedures. Stay overnight if you can so that if she wakes up, you are there to answer her cries and comfort her rather than an unfamiliar nurse. Also, offer to be the one to feed her rather than someone on the hospital staff.

Some doctors will try to discourage you from staying overnight by telling you that your child cries more when you are around. This may very well be true, because she has figured out that you are more responsive to her cries than the hospital staff.

Years ago when my son was quite young and had to be hospitalized, I insisted upon remaining with him during his stay in the hospital. The staff was opposed to the idea, either because it seemed too inconvenient or unconventional. Because I had the right professional affiliations, though, I was able to have my way. I believe that my presence there helped very much to make the experience a less threatening one for him. Today there are, fortunately, more and more hospitals which permit this practice as a matter of course, and I strongly urge you to choose the hospital on this basis.

Another medical problem parents often consult me about is colic. Their babies suffer from severe abdominal pain that persists, which makes them cry for several hours at a stretch. Some doctors believe that colic is caused by the inability of the child's digestive system to handle food because the opening between the stomach and the intestine may not be big enough for the food to pass through easily. Colic is usually accompanied by a vigorous cry not unlike the cry you may hear when a baby is angry, and it occurs regularly during the day or at night.

If you suspect that your baby suffers from colic, have your doctor examine him, and give as complete a history as you can of what foods your baby has been fed. Sometimes a child develops a food or other allergy that manifests itself as stomach discomfort. By eliminating that particular food, you eliminate the condition.

If it is colic, however, there is really little you can do to relieve the discomfort. It is therefore a very trying problem for the infant and his parents. You may, out of desperation, feel like giving up, but don't. When he begins to cry, your inclination may be to pick him up and walk around, or simply hold him. Some doctors will advise you to put him down after a little while if this does not seem to help, but I would much prefer to have you follow your instincts.

It's true that holding him does not provide a solution to the actual problem, but colic is something that goes away very abruptly, usually by three months of age. If you have done your best to comfort your baby and let him know you were aware of his pain, he will adjust far more easily than the child who has been ignored. Children who have been held and cuddled frequently turn out to be wonderfully happy and outgoing once the colic subsides. They will not have been spoiled by the extra attention.

Crib death or "Sudden Infant Death Syndrome" (S.I.D.S.) is a source of great anxiety for parents. In the United States there are probably somewhere around ten thousand babies a year who die of S.I.D.S. To say that there was nothing wrong with these babies is incorrect and has caused parents who lost a child to S.I.D.S. enormous guilt. They often blame themselves for the death of an infant who supposedly had nothing organically wrong with him.

Fortunately we are now beginning to understand more and more about the causes. S.I.D.S. occurs in the first six months of life. What basically happens is that the baby stops breathing while he is asleep. Most babies normally breathe in an uneven pattern, and parents should not get anxious if, during the course of the night, they hear their baby breathing fitfully.

Research being conducted on the disease points to four factors which seem to have a strong bearing on S.I.D.S. These are: mothers who smoke while pregnant, severe maternal anemia during pregnancy, a sudden lowering of blood pressure during the final trimester of the pregnancy, and premature delivery. The common element which seems to be the link to S.I.D.S. is that all four conditions cause a decrease in the delivery of oxygen during the pregnancy.

Good prenatal care is particularly important in the prevention of S.I.D.S. Pregnant women who suspect that they are anemic should be checked for the condition; if it is present, it should be treated immediately. Women who smoke should by all means stop, at least during pregnancy.

S.I.D.S. seems to occur more frequently during the winter months. Respiratory infections are more common during this period, and this may somehow contribute to the syndrome, which appears more among low-weight babies who seem more sensitive to other environmental conditions as well.

Although I would counsel you not to worry unduly about S.I.D.S., it is one reason why some parents prefer to have their baby sleep in their room—especially during the first six months, which is when virtually all the cases seem to occur. S.I.D.S. is a relatively rare occurrence, but it is certainly a tragic one. The tragedy is often compounded by people who, consciously or unconsciously, imply that there might have been something the bereaved parents could have done to prevent their baby's death. The reality is that an abnormality was present that could not have been detected. Research is currently being conducted to learn more about preventing it.

Teething is very much a part of every baby's first year. Few children experience little or no discomfort, some have occasional bouts of unhappiness, but most suffer considerable pain and may even be more prone to colds and fever as the teeth push through the gums. When babies tend to drool more it is a sure sign that they are beginning to teethe.

I recently attended a family get-together at a restaurant at which a young infant was also present. During dinner she became rather fretful, although she had recently been fed, and her parents' attempts to quiet her were not getting much success. I offered to hold her and noticed that she was drooling quite a bit. Thinking she was probably beginning to teethe and was therefore feeling a little bit of pain, I gently began to rub her gums with my finger (having made sure, of course, that it was clean). Her irritation subsided and, to her parents' amazement, she relaxed in my arms.

When your baby bites down on your nipple or the nipple of her bottle, she may be letting you know that she needs to bite to alleviate the pressure on her gums because she is starting to teethe. Rubbing her gums or offering her a teething ring may help relieve the distress somewhat. There are teething rings available that are kept in the refrigerator so that the coldness of the rubber contributes to numbing the pain. Check with your doctor if your baby seems to be in considerable discomfort; perhaps he can recommend some mild medication. You and your baby will survive the worst of the teething process; but, more importantly, do continue to respond to her cries and to give her the attention she demands and needs.

I happen not to worry much about thumbsucking. Even babies whose sucking

needs have been satisfied sometimes suck their thumbs when they are frightened or tired or about to fall asleep. Some babies who have not had enough oral stimulation may be more inclined to continue sucking for a longer period of time. It is a perfectly acceptable form of regressive behavior, a way of going back to that infantile state when they related to the world by putting almost everything in their mouths.

During the first few months of life when babies accidentally touch their faces to something, they automatically open their mouths and latch on to whatever happens to be right there. This is called a rooting response. If it is their hand, they will begin to suck on that. I don't consider thumbsucking a cause for worry. But if you feel uncomfortable about it, you can gently take your child's hand out

of her mouth if you find she has fallen asleep with it there. Sometimes this works to offset the development of the thumbsucking habit.

I am absolutely opposed to the use of bitter substances to break the thumbsucking habit. By the time a thumbsucking child reaches first or second grade, in all likelihood other children may have teased her out of it. Parents, on the other hand, should not tease a child about it.

Dentists will tell you that thumbsucking can cause malformations of the mouth. While this is sometimes true, I think it is easier to straighten a child's teeth than it is to undo emotional problems caused by making an issue of thumbsucking. In most instances, any damage that may occur will happen only if a child sucks her thumb constantly.

You will find many babies, thumbsuckers or not, who adopt a favorite stuffed animal, a blanket, or a piece of cloth from which they cannot bear to be parted. Psychologists call them transitional objects, and they help children feel more comfortable as they go off to sleep or when they are under pressure. It is as if they are taking part of the waking world with them to the unknown world of sleep. It's not uncommon for a child to save whatever he can of his special blanket, even if it is in shreds after it's been laundered time and again. I know of a few very successful adults who have not yet given up their beloved childhood toy, blanket, or pillow. If your baby has such an object, I would certainly recommend that you do nothing to take it away from him. Allow him the pleasure of its companionship.

Over the years I have been approached with questions about child rearing by many people. In the course of my discussion it appeared that the parents had dealt with the problems correctly. What I learned subsequently was that they needed support for their approach because some close relative—in most cases one of their own parents—had caused them to doubt their judgment.

Grandparents are marvelous and children are very fortunate if they have grandparents who are involved in their care. From a very early age most children love their grandparents, who tend to indulge them and give them whatever they want whenever they want it. The relationship between grandparents and grandchildren is a very special one.

Grandparents can also be a tremendous help to you. I think it's important to recognize, though, that if you are going to ask your parents to babysit or help you, you will have to accept the fact that they may then want to come and go to your house whenever it pleases them. I have heard grandparents complain, "They always call me whenever they need me—but when I want to come over they tell me they're busy."

Some grandparents want to take over. They have very strong, fixed ideas that they want to impose on you. Keep in mind that you are the baby's parents, and you have primary responsibility. You are entitled to have your opinions and to follow your own instincts in raising your baby.

Don't allow your parents to undermine your confidence by constantly telling you how to do things. This kind of pressure can sometimes lead to marital discord. While you may be willing to listen to your parents, your spouse may not be so willing. Grandparents can be very, very helpful, but be careful how you include them in your life.

While this does not apply now, during your child's first year, as your child gets older grandparents take on a different kind of role. They may be inclined, for example, to let grandchildren jump all over things, do whatever they want, and otherwise violate rules. When your child points this out to you, don't hesitate to say, "It's okay to do these things in Grandma and Grandpa's house, but not here at home."

On occasion a grandparent will inadvertently engage in a conspiracy with your child, which may undermine your authority, by saying, for example, "Here's some bubble gum, darling. Just don't tell your mother because I know she doesn't want you to have it, and I'll get in trouble." This is awful; it teaches children to conspire and do things behind your back. You sometimes have to establish rules and regulations with your parents that are not unlike those you establish for your children.

You may find that Grandma thinks it is more important to clean the baby in the bath than to have the baby enjoy herself, splashing and playing with her toys. I know of one grandmother who caused her infant granddaughter to panic every time she was faced with a bath because Grandma insisted on washing the baby's face and ears until they were squeaky clean, to the point that the baby was in pain from the scrubbing. The grandmother was sure the child would eventually forget her fear, but in fact this sort of treatment caused her great tension every time she knew she was about to be bathed, and led to a very severe fear of water which carried into the teen years.

Some grandparents are very superstitious. There is nothing wrong with this, unless, by transmitting their beliefs, they frighten the baby or prevent you from doing something that seems to you not only altogether acceptable but beneficial. Sometimes your parents tend to be more cautious than you because when they were raising their children there were fewer modern conveniences and far greater health hazards. Children today are vaccinated and therefore protected against

107

diseases that used to kill them. We now have antibiotics to cure illnesses that formerly contributed to a high infant mortality rate.

There are grandparents who feel a baby should be started on toilet training quite early in his life. This notion is not only absurd but can be psychologically harmful. They may consider it a great gift to you to toilet train your nine-month-old while you are not there, and may not tell you about it in advance. Toilet training at this age can be severely traumatic to a baby. This is why you must talk out with the grandparents what your philosophy is. I do not mean to imply that I disagree with the way grandparents do things. They have, after all, had a great deal of experience raising children. But they must respect you enough as a parent to accept you and your ways. There is nothing wrong with them letting you know how they might go about doing something, as long as they do so in a way that doesn't undermine your confidence.

9

COPING WITH SIBLING RIVALRY

SIBLING RIVALRY, jealousy, and resentment may occur between brothers and sisters, and is one of the issues that concerns most parents I have talked with. While sibling rivalry is quite common, I do not believe it exists among all siblings. I have met many brothers and sisters who genuinely like and love one another, who play happily together with a minimum of normal arguments, and who grow up into adults who enjoy one another's company.

Many children, whether related or not, will compete for the time and interest of the adults who are there to take care of them, particularly if there is little adult attention being offered in the first place. They will also fight over who gets to play with a favorite toy, who chooses which book to read, and whose turn it is to perform some coveted task. This is true within a family, in school, at summer camp, or the cub scout meeting. Every child wants the full attention of the responsible adult, particularly in the case of parents, when he has reason to assume that the adult will fill whatever his needs are. Often the rivalry children exhibit outside the family is just as fierce and as meaningful as it is within the family. However, within the family structure it implies something different. A child may feel he has lost out by having a brother or sister, that he now has a rival for your affec-

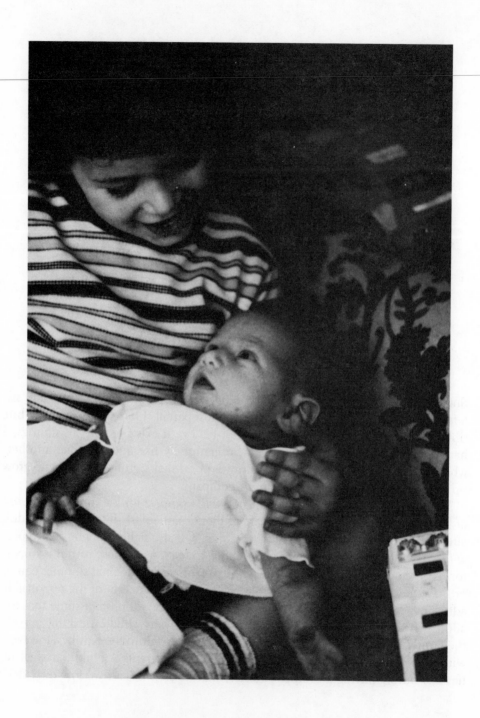

tion. The more loved a child feels, the less inclined he is to be jealous or envious of a sibling.

If parents have satisfied a child's emotional needs up to the point when a new baby suddenly becomes a part of the family, that older child has every right to expect that his needs will continue to be met. When these expectations are disappointed, he will very likely begin to resent and feel hostility toward his new sibling. Not only is he no longer getting his parents' attention, but he sees that it is now being directed at someone he cannot help but perceive as an unwelcome intruder. If, however, his parents continue to meet his demands and show that they love him very much despite the fact that they are involved with the new baby, he won't feel that he has lost anything or that the infant in his parent's arms is an enemy.

I believe it is crucially important for parents to prepare the older child for the birth of a baby and to be honest, direct, and concrete in their explanations of what will take place. How much and what you tell certainly depends on how old your child is and how much he understands. Children are sensitive to what is going on around them, and they cannot help but notice that some change is taking place. Tell your child that you are going to have a baby at the same time that you are telling everyone else. Include him in the planning and discussions. If he begins to feel left out even before his sibling is born, you are already giving him cause to look upon the baby as a rival.

Explain that the baby will be very little and won't be able to do much for a while, and that because of this the baby won't be able to play with him. As your child tries to assimilate the situation, he will wonder: Why are you having this new baby? What will he or she be like? Will he like the baby? Will you still like him? His reactions probably range from excitement and eagerness about having someone to play with to anger and hurt that you feel the need for another child.

This is why it is so important to talk to him and explain things. Help him make sense of this change in the family structure and get used to the idea. He is entitled to his own emotions, even if they are negative, and his ambivalence is perfectly normal. Allow him to express doubts and let him know it is all right to feel that way, even after the child is born.

Why paint a rosy picture of how much fun he will have with his little brother or sister and how much he will love him when at this point he hasn't even met the new baby?

At some point toward the end of the pregnancy, explain to your child that when the baby is ready to be born, you will have to go into the hospital where a doctor will help the baby get born. Let him know that you will spend several days there resting before coming home with the baby. Ideally, he should be allowed to visit you there and see the new baby. I believe that every hospital should permit young children to visit their mothers in the hospital and to meet their new brothers and sisters.

Children have marvelous, sometimes lurid imaginations. It's often hard to know how they translate the information we share with them. No matter how clear and exact a description you think you may have given of the delivery process, a child can nevertheless envision you lying helpless and cut open. He imagines that you have forgotten all about him and that you are only interested in the new baby. If he can see that you are feeling fine, have not forgotten him, and are able to walk around and hug him, it may be very comforting.

Unfortunately, some hospitals still prohibit young children from coming to visit a mother and new baby. Understandably, the older sibling will be annoyed and resentful if he knows that Grandma, Grandpa, his aunts and uncles, and even people who are just acquaintances can visit his mother and baby sister, but he can't. Some people will protest that it is more upsetting for a child to visit his mother for an hour or two and then have to say good-bye and leave without her. I think that if he knows he can return every day until his mother and sibling come home, the separation will not be as traumatic as it is when he is separated from his mother altogether for several days.

When mother and baby finally do come home, parents should be prepared for negative feelings on the part of the older child. You know how much of your energy has to go into meeting a baby's demands, but your youngster will probably feel that now that mother is home again, he has every right to expect an extra amount of attention. Try to give him that time and attention to forestall having him demand it by acting negatively or doing destructive things. Spend time alone with him whenever you can and, above all, accept his feelings.

Don't coerce him into expressions of affection and tenderness for his new sibling. These emotions will eventually develop. He really does need time to get used to such a new situation and to convince himself that, despite the new addition, he is as important to you as he ever was. It's important to accept the fact that your older child may at first resent or even hate the baby. Don't be shocked if he announces to you, two weeks after the baby is born, "Take him back to the hospital. We don't want him anymore." Rather than trying to reason with or persuade him you might say, "I know you don't like him and that's all right, but you are not allowed to hurt him."

It is not uncommon for a toilet-trained four-year-old to start wetting his pants again after the new baby comes home. He may decide he wants to drink from a bottle or your breast just like your newborn does. Or you may discover him in the baby's crib, curled up just like his baby brother.

These are all signals to you that your child is having some difficulty with the new baby's presence. He is telling you he is jealous of the attention you are giving his sibling and is prepared to surrender his status of "big boy" and act like a baby if that's what is necessary to have you pay more attention to him. Rather than becoming angry and impatient, respond to his message by giving him the individual time and attention he is asking for. Let him know he does not have to act like a baby in order to continue to be loved by you.

It's a good idea for one parent or the other to take the older child off alone to do things from time to time. Not everything has to be done with the whole family together. If the older child, who has been an only child for a while now, has to share everything with the baby and never has private time with the parents, he has some good reason for his feelings of resentment. Show respect for the older child's feelings and for his desire to keep some of those precious moments that he has always had with you. His adjustment to the new baby will be much easier.

The way in which the parents handle matters between their children sometimes leads to intense sibling rivalry. One mother, describing the jealousy and anger of her three-year-old toward his nine-month-old brother, explained to me how upset she was. She couldn't understand why he had such feelings of resentment and was constantly accusing her of loving the baby more than she loved him or of not loving him at all.

In discussing the situation with her, I learned that she constantly compared the two children. One such episode took place at the dinner table when both children were eating. She had given her older child a lamb chop and peas and was feeding the baby creamed vegetables. When the older child refused to finish his peas, the mother said, "Look at how nicely your baby brother is eating his vegetables. Why can't you be as good an eater as he is?" The little boy slammed his hand on the table, shattered his plate, and ran out of the room in tears, screaming, "You don't love me!"

No matter how much this mother tried to convince the child that she did love him, he interpreted her comparison of him to his brother as rejection. Her criticism was particularly hurtful, since no three-year-old cares to be compared with a baby. Such comparisons can create and increase sibling rivalry where none might otherwise exist.

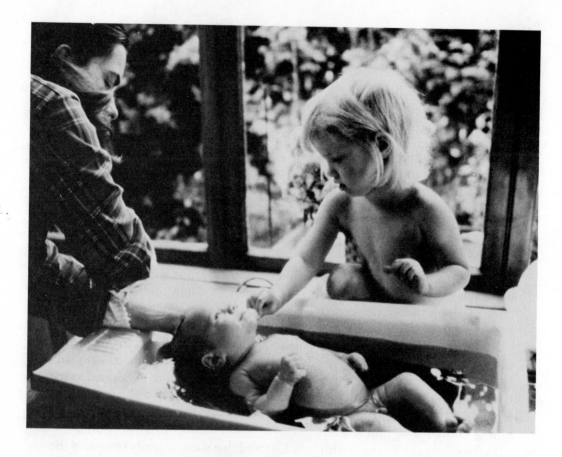

Some parents have been told by pediatricians or others who give them advice about child rearing that when people come to visit the new baby and bring him a present, they should have something available to give to the older child so she will not feel left out. I disagree with this approach because the message you are giving the older child is that every time the baby gets a gift, she is also entitled to something. This is totally unrealistic and nobody should grow up expecting such equal treatment. Not only is it impossible to carry out, but it is bound to lead to disappointment. It's far better to help the older child learn to come to terms with the fact that she and the baby are different and won't necessarily be treated the same way. Explain that grownups make a big fuss and bother about little babies, and that when she was born people brought her presents, too. Assure the child that you love her and the baby just as much, but in different ways because they are different people. Demonstrate your love for her by showing affection.

Not all sibling rivalry consists of the older child resenting the younger. Young children often show hostility toward their big brothers and sisters. Parents may seem to be more interested in the older child and more involved in his activities. The younger child may begin to feel as if she is left out of a family triangle formed before she was born.

A little sister may resent the fact that her older brother is allowed to cross the street alone and visit a friend who lives a mile away, whereas she is not allowed to do so. You have to make it very clear that you do not feel she is old enough to do this by herself and that as soon as she is, you will certainly allow her to. This may be more of an attempt on the part of the younger child to gain independence and freedom than an expression of sibling rivalry.

Younger children often look up to their older brothers and sisters, and express that admiration by wanting to spend a lot of time with them, playing with their friends and their toys. Parents who allow this to happen are bound to wind up with a resentful older child. After all, why should he always have his little brother tagging along? He needs to develop his own friendships outside the home and without a little brother around.

You can avoid this conflict by telling your older child that you understand his feelings and that you do not expect him to include his sibling all or even most of the time. But explain that his little brother wants to be just like him, because he looks up to him for his abilities and accomplishments. You can suggest that from time to time it would be nice to involve his little brother in his fun. In this way you are giving him a chance to do something he knows will make you happy and can also allow him to feel like a hero to his younger sibling.

Dealing with sibling rivalry is indeed difficult for parents. As is the case with many other human problems, it is far easier to prevent than to treat. Parental attitudes sometimes play a role in causing rivalry. Showing favoritism, being overly critical of one child, making comparisons, or using one child as an example to the other are ways in which parents sometimes intensify rivalry. Children who have been neglected often displace their anger from the parents to their siblings by treating them maliciously.

One way of minimizing sibling rivalry is to plan your family so that your children are born three years or more apart. That in and of itself won't necessarily prevent sibling rivalry, but it certainly makes it easier to avoid for a number of reasons.

Under the age of three most children go through a normal period of being rather negative and defiant. They are very demanding of their parents, they still need a great deal of attention, and they tend to assert themselves in a negative way. It's common for two-year-olds to be "nasty." That's why we sometimes refer to this period as "the terrible twos."

Bringing home a baby when a child is going through this stage is certainly going to increase your difficulties as a parent in being able to handle the needs of a newborn as well as those of a child who is in the throes of the terrible twos.

Children who are three years or older and have passed this negative stage can begin to learn how to share and are less dependent on their parents for full-time attention. They are generally weaned and toilet-trained by that time and are ready for a daily nursery school to help them build a life of their own.

A child under the age of three has a very hard time understanding the concept of a new baby—how the baby is conceived and born. After the age of three children are generally naturally curious about the subject and are more capable of understanding the process of reproduction and birth.

Each child wants to be thought of as an individual, to be accepted on his own merits and without comparison to anyone else. As long as a child is sure that you love him for himself, he will have less reason to look at a sibling as a threat to his security. This is true, by the way, of multiple birth siblings. No matter how much twins look alike, they are separate persons and generally very aware of their differences. If they themselves express a desire to dress alike or to pursue the same interests, by all means allow them to do so. Respect their individuality, even if their individuality involves their doing similar things or dressing alike. On the other hand, give them the freedom to develop their own distinctive personalities.

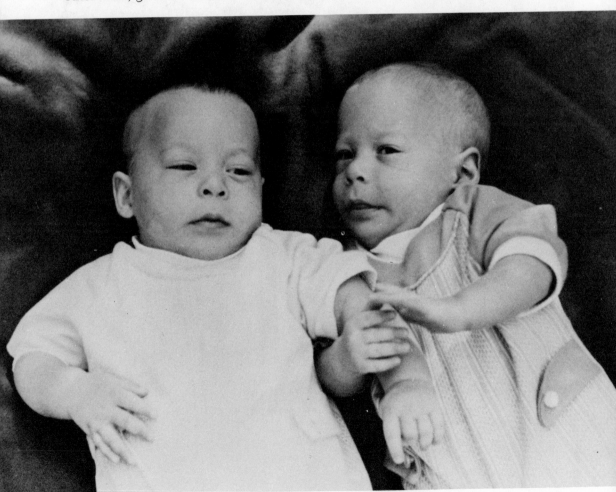

LOOKING AHEAD

Now that I have taken you through the major problems, concerns, and experiences that you are likely to encounter in your child's first year of life, it is my hope that you have not been overwhelmed by what I have had to say. I truly believe that the joys and satisfactions you will receive during this and the many years to come will far outweigh any of the problems and anguish you may occasionally experience. You are indeed important in your baby's life—I cannot emphasize this too much!

In much the same way that I have enjoyed being a very active and involved parent in raising my two children, I hope that you will also have those satisfactions. Consider this first year of your child's life as an investment not only in the future of your child, but in the future of our world. Raising happy, healthy, and fulfilled children is more than personally gratifying. Emotionally secure children will be able to pass on that security to their children and their children's children. Therefore, consider whatever you give your child as going far beyond his or her own life, because it will be transmitted to future generations.

INDEX

PICTURE CREDITS